D0945760

12

Current
CONTROVERSIES

Modern-Day Piracy

DATE DUE

DISCARD

GAYLORD   PRINTED IN U.S.A.

Other Books in the Current Controversies Series

Modern-Day Piracy

Debra A. Miller, Book Editor

GREENHAVEN PRESS

A part of Gale, Cengage Learning

OAKTON COMMUNITY COLLEGE
DES PLAINES CAMPUS
1600 EAST GOLF ROAD
DES PLAINES, IL 60016

GALE
CENGAGE Learning·

Detroit • New York • San Francisco • New Haven, Conn • Waterville, Maine • London

Elizabeth Des Chenes, *Managing Editor*

© 2012 Greenhaven Press, a part of Gale, Cengage Learning

Gale and Greenhaven Press are registered trademarks used herein under license.

For more information, contact:
Greenhaven Press
27500 Drake Rd.
Farmington Hills, MI 48331-3535
Or you can visit our Internet site at gale.cengage.com

ALL RIGHTS RESERVED.
No part of this work covered by the copyright herein may be reproduced, transmitted, stored, or used in any form or by any means graphic, electronic, or mechanical, including but not limited to photocopying, recording, scanning, digitizing, taping, Web distribution, information networks, or information storage and retrieval systems, except as permitted under Section 107 or 108 of the 1976 United States Copyright Act, without the prior written permission of the publisher.

For product information and technology assistance, contact us at

Gale Customer Support, 1-800-877-4253
For permission to use material from this text or product, submit all requests online at www.cengage.com/permissions

Further permissions questions can be emailed to permissionrequest@cengage.com

Articles in Greenhaven Press anthologies are often edited for length to meet page require-ments. In addition, original titles of these works are changed to clearly present the main thesis and to explicitly indicate the author's opinion. Every effort is made to ensure that Greenhaven Press accurately reflects the original intent of the authors. Every effort has been made to trace the owners of copyrighted material.

Cover image copyright © Presselect/Alamy.

LIBRARY OF CONGRESS CATALOGING-IN-PUBLICATION DATA

Modern-day piracy / Debra A. Miller, book editor.
    p. cm. -- (Current controversies)
    Includes bibliographical references and index.
    ISBN 978-0-7377-6028-6 (hbk.) -- ISBN 978-0-7377-6029-3 (pbk.)
    1. Pirates--Somalia--21st century. 2. Hijacking of ships--Somalia--21st century. 3. Maritime terrorism--Somalia--21st century. 4. Piracy--Prevention. 5. Piracy--Prevention--Government policy. 6. Shipping--Security measures. 7. Merchant marine--Security measures. I. Miller, Debra A. II. Series: Current controversies.
    DT403.2.M63 2012
    364.16'4--dc23

                            2011042045

Printed in the United States of America
1 2 3 4 5   16 15 14 13 12
FD055

Contents

DISCARD

Piracy re-emerged in various areas of the world in the 1990s, but in the last few years more than half the pirate attacks have occurred in the waters off the Horn of Africa. The number of pirate attacks in this region nearly doubled between 2008 and 2009—from 111 to 217—and attacks have continued since. At first Somali pirates attacked ships sailing close to Somalia's coast, but as ships have moved further out to sea, the pirates have followed, taking hostages for ransom and becoming ever more sophisticated in their operations.

Chapter 2: Is Piracy Connected to Terrorism?

Given the increase in piracy off the coast of Somalia in recent years, combined with the rise of an Islamist movement in the country, security officials worry about the risks of maritime terrorism affecting world trade. Although reliable information is hard to find, the weight of current evidence strongly suggests that Somalia pirates are motivated by economic rather than terrorist motives.

Rumors have spread that Somali pirates pay commissions to al-Shabaab, a Somalia-based Islamist group with ties to terrorism, and that al-Shabaab helps to arm and train the pirates. The truth is, however, that al-Shabaab disapproves of pirate operations because they interfere with the group's main source of income—port taxes and shipments of goods. There is no proof that piracy is linked to terrorism.

Chapter 3: Should Ransoms Be Paid to Pirates?

In 2011, the United States changed its policy concerning piracy and decided not to pay a ransom, instead having navy snipers fatally shoot three pirates holding an American ship's captain hostage. Although this effort freed the captain, this more aggressive stance toward piracy will likely remove the economic incentive for pirates to treat hostages humanely, encourage pirates to become more violent, and endanger the lives of future hostages.

There are very few options available to governments when ships are hijacked because of the risk of endangering the lives of the crew held hostage onboard. Given the lack of a satisfactory public response, paying ransoms is the only way a ship owner can retrieve its ship and cargo, obtain release of hostages, and avoid the risk of environmental disasters such as oil spills.

According to Illinois Senator Mark Kirk, the United States should ban the payment of ransoms to Somali pirates and should encourage a policy that allows merchant ships to carry arms in order to defend themselves against pirate attacks. This strategy could pose a risk to the hundreds of hostages currently being held by pirates, but it is the best way to put an end to piracy.

Chapter 4: How Should the US and Other Nations Combat Pirate Attacks?

The Barack Obama administration must resist calling for immediate actions against pirates and terrorists in Somalia and focus instead on helping Somalis establish a stable nation. This means supporting the current efforts toward democratic elections and creating a moderate Islamic government in Somalia, so that it can fight piracy and the threat of terrorism within its borders.

Foreword

By definition, controversies are "discussions of questions in which opposing opinions clash" (*Webster's Twentieth Century Dictionary Unabridged*). Few would deny that controversies are a pervasive part of the human condition and exist on virtually every level of human enterprise. Controversies transpire between individuals and among groups, within nations and between nations. Controversies supply the grist necessary for progress by providing challenges and challengers to the status quo. They also create atmospheres where strife and warfare can flourish. A world without controversies would be a peaceful world; but it also would be, by and large, static and prosaic.

The Series' Purpose

The purpose of the Current Controversies series is to explore many of the social, political, and economic controversies dominating the national and international scenes today. Titles selected for inclusion in the series are highly focused and specific. For example, from the larger category of criminal justice, Current Controversies deals with specific topics such as police brutality, gun control, white collar crime, and others. The debates in Current Controversies also are presented in a useful, timeless fashion. Articles and book excerpts included in each title are selected if they contribute valuable, long-range ideas to the overall debate. And wherever possible, current information is enhanced with historical documents and other relevant materials. Thus, while individual titles are current in focus, every effort is made to ensure that they will not become quickly outdated. Books in the Current Controversies series will remain important resources for librarians, teachers, and students for many years.

In addition to keeping the titles focused and specific, great care is taken in the editorial format of each book in the series. Book introductions and chapter prefaces are offered to provide background material for readers. Chapters are organized around several key questions that are answered with diverse opinions representing all points on the political spectrum. Materials in each chapter include opinions in which authors clearly disagree as well as alternative opinions in which authors may agree on a broader issue but disagree on the possible solutions. In this way, the content of each volume in Current Controversies mirrors the mosaic of opinions encountered in society. Readers will quickly realize that there are many viable answers to these complex issues. By questioning each author's conclusions, students and casual readers can begin to develop the critical thinking skills so important to evaluating opinionated material.

Current Controversies is also ideal for controlled research. Each anthology in the series is composed of primary sources taken from a wide gamut of informational categories including periodicals, newspapers, books, US and foreign government documents, and the publications of private and public organizations. Readers will find factual support for reports, debates, and research papers covering all areas of important issues. In addition, an annotated table of contents, an index, a book and periodical bibliography, and a list of organizations to contact are included in each book to expedite further research.

Perhaps more than ever before in history, people are confronted with diverse and contradictory information. During the Persian Gulf War, for example, the public was not only treated to minute-to-minute coverage of the war, it was also inundated with critiques of the coverage and countless analyses of the factors motivating US involvement. Being able to sort through the plethora of opinions accompanying today's major issues, and to draw one's own conclusions, can be a complicated and frustrating struggle. It is the editors' hope that Current Controversies will help readers with this struggle.

Introduction

> *"The reality is that pirates are thieves who prey on unarmed ships to steal their cargoes and kidnappers who hold ships and their crews hostage in order to procure hefty ransoms."*

Movies and television shows typically portray pirates as romantic, swashbuckling, and often heroic figures, but the reality is that pirates are thieves who prey on unarmed ships to steal their cargoes and kidnappers who hold ships and their crews hostage in order to procure hefty ransoms. This crime of piracy is an age-old phenomenon, dating back as far as there are records of sailing the high seas, but a so-called golden age of piracy occurred during the 1600s and 1700s, when the practice flourished in the Caribbean and Mediterranean seas. Although piracy declined significantly during the 1800s and thereafter, it has re-emerged in recent decades, particularly in the waters off the Horn of Africa, near the poor and politically unstable nation of Somalia.

Piracy began thousands of years ago when civilizations took to the seas for trade and conquest. Ships belonging to the ancient Greeks and Romans came under attack, for example, and the Vikings earned a reputation for sea-based aggression against both ships and coastal communities. Beginning in the early 1600s, however, piracy became much more commonplace, as both private and government-authorized pirates attacked ships on the high seas and in coastal regions. Many pirates at this time were privateers, seamen who were issued letters of marque from governments in Europe, giving them permission to plunder ships of other nations. The profits would then be shared between the privateer and the government. One of the most famous privateers was Sir Francis

Drake—a sea captain who was commissioned by Queen Elizabeth I to raid Spanish ships returning from the New World with treasures. Drake was acclaimed as a hero in Britain but was viewed as a criminal by Spain. Also during this period, pirates and privateers called buccaneers attacked ships in the Caribbean Sea from bases in the West Indies, and Muslim pirates called corsairs were sent by governments of countries in North Africa to attack the ships of Christian countries in the Mediterranean.

In fact, probably the most famous pirates in history were the Barbary pirates of North Africa, who ruled the Mediterranean Sea during the late 1700s. Pirate ships from the North African states of Tripoli, Tunis, Morocco, and Algiers—an area known as the Barbary Coast—routinely attacked European and American merchant ships unless a bribe, called a tribute, was paid to the pirate nations guaranteeing safe passage. The profits realized from these tributes and pirate attacks were a primary source of income to these African nations. For many years, European countries paid these tributes rather than risk attacks, and before and during the American Revolution, Britain and France paid tributes to the pirate nations to protect American ships and sailors. But once the United States won its independence from Britain, it was responsible to pay its own tribute to the Barbary states, which it did in 1784 in the amount of eighty thousand dollars.

The following year, however, marked a turning point in America's policy toward Barbary piracy. In July 1785, after the United States had failed to pay tribute, Algerians captured two American ships and held their crews hostage. George Washington, America's first president, tried to negotiate with the Barbary countries but to no avail. Thomas Jefferson, then US ambassador to France, argued strenuously against the payment of tributes or ransoms, but he was unsuccessful in getting European countries to form a naval coalition to fight piracy. As a result, years later a ransom of almost a million dollars was paid for the return of the US ships and crew, and America continued to pay tributes during the next presidential term of John Adams.

After Jefferson became president in 1801, he was determined to take a different course. The ruler of Tripoli demanded an outrageous payment of $225,000 plus an annual tribute of $25,000, but Jefferson refused to pay any more tributes, instead sending a fleet of US naval ships to the region. Jefferson's show of force helped to calm the threat of piracy for a time, until the American ship *Philadelphia* was captured by pirates in Tripoli in 1803. This pirate victory, in turn, unleashed a new American naval and marine operation against Tripoli, this time with the goal of overturning its leadership. The United States won this first Barbary war, installed a new ruler, and signed a treaty with Tripoli in 1806 that restrained the pirates for the next decade. Barbary piracy was not fully banished, however, until the United States won a second Barbary war in 1815, leading to treaties ending US tributes to all the Barbary states.

Following the vanquishing of the Barbary pirates, piracy ceased to be a major problem for shipping nations for most of the nineteenth and twentieth centuries. But during the 1990s, pirate attacks once again began to increase. According to the International Maritime Bureau, an international body that tracks pirate attacks, the number of pirate attacks tripled during the period of 1993 to 2003, and since then have continued to increase each year. In 2010, 445 pirate attacks were reported, and pirates captured fifty-three ships and a total of 1,181 hostages—a 10 percent increase from 2009. The most dangerous place for modern pirate attacks is in the waters off Somalia, a desperately poor and politically unstable nation in North Africa that has been unable to police its own territorial waters or prosecute Somalian pirates responsible for attacks. In recent years, despite the establishment of international naval patrols, Somali pirates have become ever more brazen, demanding higher and higher ransoms, and in some cases re-sorting to violence against hostages.

The problem of modern piracy is the subject of *Current Controversies: Modern-Day Piracy*. Authors in this volume address a number of critical questions, such as the scope of today's piracy, whether there is a connection between pirates and terrorists, whether ransoms should be paid, and how the United States and the rest of the international community should respond to pirate attacks.

CHAPTER 1

What Is the Scope of Today's Maritime Piracy?

Chapter Preface

Most experts agree that piracy around Somalia is rooted in the poverty and political instability that has plagued that nation in North Africa for the last two decades. The best hope of improving the situation appears to be the Transitional Federal Government (TFG), an internationally recognized entity that seeks to create a functional government and to improve security and economic conditions in Somalia. The United States and other nations have supported the TFG's efforts in the hopes of finding a long-term solution to Somali piracy, but the international community has also pursued short-term responses to the pirate problem. The main short-term response to date has been the creation of a multinational naval flotilla that patrols the waters off Somalia to deter and respond to pirate attacks.

The naval antipiracy force was authorized by the Security Council, the United Nations (UN) governing body, in 2008 under UN Resolutions 1816 and 1851, to carry out antipiracy operations in Somalian territorial waters and on land. Both resolutions require that any antipiracy actions be carried out with the consent of the TFG and be undertaken in accordance with humanitarian and human rights laws. Other UN resolutions authorize the provision of training and technical assistance to TFG forces to help them improve maritime security. Under UN authority, US, North Atlantic Treaty Organization (NATO), European Union (EU), regional, and other naval forces are currently patrolling near Somalia.

Some of these naval forces are operating as part of an organization called Combined Task Force, or CTF-151. This force was created on January 8, 2009, by the US military and is made up of navy components from not only the United States but also Denmark, Turkey, and Singapore. It was originally commanded by the United States, but command has now passed to the Turkish Navy. In addition to CTF-151 is an EU maritime security force called EU Naval Force Operation Atalanta. This force consists of naval forces from Belgium, France, Germany, Greece, Italy, Luxembourg, the Netherlands, Spain, and Sweden, but other countries such as Norway, Cyprus, Ireland, Malta, and Finland are contributing personnel as well. NATO has also deployed maritime forces to conduct antipiracy operations in the Somalia area. The first such deployment, in 2008, was called Operation Allied Provider and served to protect international food assistance shipments in the region—a mission that is now performed by the EU Operation Atalanta. In 2009, NATO launched other antipiracy missions; the first was called Operation Allied Protector and its replacement was Operation Ocean Shield. One important focus of these NATO operations is working with regional governments to try to improve local maritime security. Finally, ships from countries such as Russia, China, and India are cooperating with these various antipiracy efforts but are not under their command.

To coordinate all of these international antipiracy efforts, in January 2009, the United States initiated the formation of the Contact Group on Piracy Off the Coast of Somalia (CGPCS). The CGPCS, made up of about sixty countries and various international organizations, pursues six goals: (1) improving information and other support to antipiracy operations; (2) coordinating antipiracy efforts; (3) strengthening judicial frameworks for the arrest, prosecution, and detention of pirates; (4) strengthening prevention efforts of commercial ships; (5) improving diplomacy and public information; and (6) tracking financial flows related to piracy. The CGPCS meets three times a year at the UN, and it has four working groups that meet regularly to develop and implement antipiracy policies.

Yet another element of coordination for antipiracy efforts was developed as a result of meetings held by the International Maritime Organization (IMO), a United Nations agency with responsibility for the safety and security of shipping. The IMO has worked to combat piracy since the late 1990s, and in 2005, it sponsored a series of meetings focusing on piracy in the Somalia region. The meetings resulted in a 2008 cooperation agreement and a 2009 Code of Conduct concerning the Repression of Piracy and Armed Robbery Against Ships in the western Indian Ocean and the Gulf of Aden. This Code of Conduct is open to all twenty-one governments in the Horn of Africa region, but it was initially signed by nine governments—Djibouti, Ethiopia, Kenya, Madagascar, Maldives, Seychelles, Somalia, United Republic of Tanzania, and Yemen. The code defines how these countries hope to cooperate in the arrest, investigation, and prosecution of pirates or suspected pirates.

Although the naval patrols have been successful at thwarting some pirate attacks, many commentators have concluded that they have been largely ineffective. The number of pirate attacks since antipiracy naval forces began their operations in 2009 has increased dramatically. Experts on this issue explain that almost all of the Somalia-related pirate attacks used to occur near Somalia in the Gulf of Aden, a relatively narrow passageway used frequently by the world's merchant ships. After the naval patrols started, however, pirates appeared to shift their operations farther out to sea, using large so-called mother ships as bases and sending out smaller, faster boats to conduct their attacks. This made the work of the naval patrols much more difficult; patrolling such a vast area, many commentators have said, is like looking for a needle in a haystack. This chapter addresses the state and other aspects of today's maritime piracy operations.

Piracy Is Flourishing in Many Key Shipping Lanes

James G. Stavridis and Richard E. LeBron

James G. Stavridis, an admiral in the US Navy, is commander of the US European Command and supreme allied commander in Europe. Richard E. LeBron, a lieutenant commander in the US Navy, serves as special assistant to Admiral Stavridis.

The goods of the world move predominantly by sea. Across that broad global commons, trade generally flows freely and well. Yet there are places today where the term "outlaw sea" applies. Piracy, sadly, flourishes in several key choke point regions of the world's sea-lanes of communications. We must tame this outlaw sea.

A Persistent Problem

To many, the word "piracy" conjures images of seventeenth- and eighteenth-century swashbuckling rebels brandishing cutlasses and flintlocks under the ominous skull-and-crossbones flag, à la Walt Disney World's "Pirates of the Caribbean" attraction. But to those who have been victims of their blades and bullets, the word invokes a darker "profession"—and one that continues today.

Pirates and corsairs of the "Golden Age of Piracy"—feared mariners with names like Barbarossa, "Calico Jack" Rackham, "Black Bart" Roberts, and Anne Bonny—have captured imaginations since early-eighteenth-century periodicals chronicled their crimes. But piracy is more than theft, rape, and murder on the high seas. It is a systemic destabilizer of international norms of commerce, economics, and trade. Piracy is also intertwined with conditions ashore. In particular, piracy in the

James G. Stavridis and Richard E. LeBron, "Taming the Outlaw Sea," *Naval War College Review*, Autumn 2010, pp. 73–77. Copyright © 2010 by U.S. Naval War College. All rights reserved. Reproduced by permission.

waters off the Horn of Africa today results from deep social, political, economic, and environmental problems in Somalia. It is the fruit of anarchy, extreme poverty, and the severe failure of the rule of law. At the pragmatic level, however, piracy is an illicit entrepreneurial pursuit whose main objective is to maximize profit.

In other words, Somali pirates are armed opportunists who stem from a permissive and enabling environment formed by a weak state and who engage in a business enterprise subject to risk-and-reward calculations that can be influenced by the international community. The international community, including various governmental and nongovernmental organizations, as well as private enterprises, has an opportunity now to work together and exert the necessary influence both at sea and ashore to shift the calculus of piracy from profitable enterprise to futile folly.

The United Nations, the European Union (EU), the African Union, the Arab League, and NATO [North Atlantic Treaty Organization] are collaborating to influence the risk-and-reward analysis of Somali pirates. A wide range of countries—including Australia, China, Djibouti, Egypt, Ethiopia, Japan, Kenya, Malaysia, New Zealand, Pakistan, Russia, Singapore, Somalia, South Korea, and Ukraine—are cooperating to broadly address the issue as well.

Though piracy manifests itself most perceptibly at sea, it is a complex and persistent land-based problem with political, social, and economic dimensions requiring a long-term, comprehensive solution. To bring about a lasting cure to the cancer of piracy, particularly off the Horn of Africa, two endeavors must be undertaken in parallel. First, the risk of failure in hijacking a vessel at sea must be increased to the point where piracy is no longer seen as an attractive and lucrative endeavor. In other words, pirates' own calculations must yield deterrent conclusions. Second, governance, stability, and security within Somalia must be so improved that less risky yet

25

reasonably profitable alternatives to piracy can be fostered both at sea and ashore. The second task is a much more challenging proposition than the first, given Somalia's fragmented and unstable state.

Capturing the Lessons of the Past

Lawlessness upon the sea is nothing new. Piracy is an ancient profession. Its history dates back to antiquity, preceding even the ancient Egyptians. Nautical bandits have plied the waves for nearly as long as people have used the seas for trade. The Lukka raiders, for example, launched raids from the coast of Asia Minor as early as the fourteenth century BC; [ancient Greek historian] Thucydides mentions pirates in his *History of the Peloponnesian War*; and [ancient Greek historian] Herodotus writes of how pirates kidnapped the poet Arion of Methymna in an attempt to steal his riches.

As is the case today in the Horn of Africa, piracy in the ancient Mediterranean world flourished when there was an absence of central control. In periods when the empire du jour—Egyptian, Greek, or Roman—was unable to maintain a strong naval presence in the large inland sea, pirate communities spread along its shores. Before the middle of the first century BC, piracy was a significant problem in the Mediterranean. As Rome's maritime trade of wheat and other commodities flourished, piracy expanded. At their height, pirates exerted dominion and control over the Mediterranean to an extent that left little room for free navigation or commerce. The economic impact was felt throughout the Roman Republic as prices of goods—particularly of wheat, vital for feeding the Roman people—grew out of control. Even young Julius Caesar was taken for ransom by Cilician pirates, around 75 BC.

It was only when Rome's power expanded to claim the whole of the Mediterranean basin—and the littorals [shores] whence pirates sailed—that piracy was eradicated from the ancient world. Gnaeus Pompeius Magnus, known to history as Pompey, was sent by the Roman people to wrest the seas from the pirates. In combating piracy, Pompey focused on the act and its source, not exclusively on the actor. Over a period of several months in 67 BC, with hundreds of ships and 120,000 soldiers, he swept the Mediterranean Sea and corralled the pirates in their strongholds ashore.

Most surrendered. They did so because the risk of death or capture at sea in future piratical attempts exceeded the potential rewards to be gained. But they surrendered also because Pompey, understanding that piracy was bred in rootlessness and social disorder, offered attractive alternatives ashore. He admitted some into the small towns of the Cilicians in Anatolia, and others he planted in the city of the Solians, also in Anatolia; to the majority he granted land in the ancient Greek province of Achaea to call their own and cultivate. With this land he afforded the former pirates an opportunity to pursue an enterprise with more acceptable risks and rewards and so helped turn the pirates into contributing Roman subjects.

[Modern pirates] brandish not cutlasses and flintlocks but AK-47s and rocket-propelled grenades and are aided by satellite phones, high-tech navigation gear, and . . . networks ashore.

Pompey, then, wiped out Mediterranean piracy by countering pirates at sea *and* by presenting former and would-be pirates with stakes in profitable and less risky enterprises ashore. Though Somali pirates are unlikely to be presented with land to call their own, Pompey's actions provide a valuable demonstration of the balanced application of hard and soft power both at sea and ashore, one that is no less relevant and wise in combating piracy today than it was more than two millenniums ago.

Control of the Sea Is Vital

Though Pompey's strategic vision and his expedition against piracy were successful, not even the mighty Roman Empire ever extinguished piracy permanently. As civilizations and empires ebbed and flowed and control of what [nineteenth-century US naval strategist] Alfred Thayer Mahan later called a "wide common" was exerted and relinquished, so too did the threat and impact of piracy fluctuate. In the early Middle Ages, the Vikings raided and plundered their way across Europe, and later corsairs from the North African "Barbary Coast" terrorized the Mediterranean Sea. Piracy also waxed and waned in the Far East and in the Caribbean, as trade grew and the tides of profit rose and fell. As merchants ventured to sea and maritime trade expanded, pirates followed, ransacking vulnerable ships and cargo; they continue to do so to this day.

Today, however, pirates chase their prey not in galleys, sloops, or schooners but in fast, open skiffs. They brandish not cutlasses and flintlocks but AK-47s and rocket-propelled grenades and are aided by satellite phones, high-tech navigation gear, and competent and continually evolving networks ashore. The last few years have witnessed a rising trend in piratical attacks around the world. In 2009, the International Maritime Bureau (IMB) reported 406 attacks, compared to 293 in 2008, 263 in 2007, and 239 in 2006. In 2009, a total of 217 incidents carried out by suspected Somali pirates were reported to the IMB, making the area off the Horn of Africa the number-one hot spot for piracy in the world. The attacks are becoming more violent, brazen, and sophisticated. The number of incidents where guns were used nearly doubled in 2009 from 2008 levels and has tripled since 2005. Somali pirates have extended their reach, threatening not only the Gulf of Aden and the east coast of Somalia but also the southern region of the Red Sea, the strait of Bab el Mandeb, and the east coast of Oman.

The attacks listed in the IMB report were wide-ranging; they included eighty attacks off the east and south coasts of Somalia, 116 in the Gulf of Aden, fifteen in the southern Red Sea, four off Oman, and one each in the Arabian Sea and Indian Ocean. In 2009, off the east coast of Africa alone, a total of 114 vessels were fired upon, forty-seven vessels were hijacked, 867 crew members taken hostage, four killed, and one missing. By comparison, throughout the rest of the world six vessels were fired upon, two were hijacked, 185 crew members were taken hostage, four were killed, and seven were missing. Since IMB figures are based on self-reporting and many attacks may go unreported, the actual figures may very well be much higher, particularly in areas where the level of international focus on piracy is lower than it currently is off the Horn of Africa.

Piracy is estimated to cost anywhere between a billion and sixteen billion dollars a year.

The year 2010 started with a bang for the twenty-four seamen of the chemical tanker *Premoni*. The ship was attacked and hijacked, and its crew taken hostage by Somali pirates in the Gulf of Aden on 1 January. As of the second week of January a total of six vessels had been successfully attacked by pirates and bandits: *Premoni*; a liquified propane gas tanker in Côte d'Ivoire's Abidjan harbor; a vehicle carrier off the Horn of Africa; and a vehicle carrier, a chemical tanker, and a bulk carrier in Southeast Asia. As of mid-April, a total of forty-eight vessels had been attacked, or attacks had been attempted against them, off Africa's eastern shores. . . .

The annual cost of piracy is not accurately recorded, but it is not trivial, even setting human costs aside. Piracy is estimated to cost anywhere between a billion and sixteen billion dollars a year. Some countries are investing to thwart piracy by increasing their military presences in high-risk areas. Some shipping companies are taking such measures as rerouting ships to bypass the Gulf of Aden, hiring private security guards, and installing nonlethal deterrence equipment. Examples of the latter are the Long Range Acoustic Device, which was employed against pirates attempting to hijack the luxury cruise ship *Seabourne Spirit* in late 2005, and Secure-Ship, an innovative electrified fence that surrounds the whole ship and uses a high-voltage pulse to deter boarding attempts. But these actions all come at a price. For example, routing a tanker from Saudi Arabia to the United States via the Cape of Good Hope [i.e., around the southern tip of Africa] adds approximately 2,700 miles to the voyage and approximately $3.5 million in annual fuel costs. According to the U.S. Maritime Administration, the cost of avoiding risk becomes more complex in the liner trades. If pirates were to become able to attack cruise liners successfully and regularly, the long bypass required to avoid them would result in the need for additional vessels to maintain scheduled service and capacity commitments. For example, routing from Europe to the Far East via the Cape of Good Hope rather than through the Suez Canal would incur an estimated additional $89 million annually—$74.4 million in fuel and $14.6 million in charter expenses—without considering the added costs associated with disruption of global supply chains. Also, insurance costs have soared over the last few years. The cost of war-risk insurance premiums for vessels passing through the Gulf of Aden, about five hundred dollars in 2007, was twenty thousand dollars in 2008. A shipowner with a vessel worth $100 million can now reportedly expect to pay about $150,000 to cover its payload—a cost that is ultimately passed on to the consumer.

Not all is bad news, however. The rate of successful hijackings in the vicinity of the Horn of Africa dropped in the second half of 2009, to an average of one in nine vessels targeted by pirates, compared to one in 6.4 in 2008. The decrease can be attributed to expanded control of the sea around the Horn of Africa established through increased international cooperation and naval patrols; expanded coordination of naval patrols through the use of the Mercury secure, Internet-based communication system; shared intelligence at the operational level; and willingness of potential target ships to respond to military guidance, comply with recommendations, and deploy effective protective measures. If continued, these measures, particularly self-protection by potential targets, will likely drive the rate of successful hijackings down further.

Attacks by Somali Pirates Have Increased in Recent Years

Raymond Gilpin

Raymond Gilpin is the director of the Center for Sustainable Economies, a project of the US Institute of Peace, an independent, nonpartisan, national institution established and funded by Congress to help end international conflicts and promote global stability and peace.

Roughly the same size of France and six times the size of the U.S. state of Virginia, Somalia has a 3,025 km coastline (longer than the U.S. portion of the Gulf of Mexico, which is some 2,700 km) on the northeastern corner of Africa. Its recent history has been marred by violence and instability. Since the fall of the Siad Barre regime in 1991, there have been more than a dozen attempts to forge political consensus and establish a functioning central government. Although the Transnational Federal Government was established in 2003, with its capital in the southern city of Mogadishu, it remains fairly ineffective. De facto, Somalia is governed by a system of clans operating in three relatively autonomous regions—Somaliland in the northwest, Puntland in the northeast and Central Somalia in the central and southern regions.

Poverty Is Rife in Somalia

Poverty and unemployment are rife in Somalia. The World Bank estimates that over 40 percent of Somalis live in extreme poverty (less than a dollar a day) and almost 75 percent of households subsist on less than $2 a day. Approximately two-

Raymond Gilpin, "Counting the Costs of Somalia Piracy," USIP.org, June 22, 2009. Copyright © 2009 by United States Institute of Peace. All rights reserved. Reproduced by permission.

thirds of Somali youth are without jobs. A combination of inter-clan rivalry, corruption, arms proliferation, extremism and pervasive impunity has facilitated crime in most parts of Somalia, particularly in Puntland and Central Somalia. This criminal activity eventually moved from land to the sea.

Somali piracy rose to global prominence with an increase in attacks during 2008, record ransom payments, and the deployment of . . . [antipiracy] naval vessels from over a dozen nations.

Clan militia made the transition to maritime crime by claiming to protect Somalia's territorial waters from poachers and polluters. Under a number of names (including: the Central Somalia Coast Guard, the National Volunteer Coast Guard, and the Somali Marines) clan militia started by forcibly levying taxes and fines on ships they managed to board. This quickly evolved to hijacking. Piracy off Somalia has now crystallized around major clans based around the coastal villages of Eyl and Garaad in Puntland, and the coastal villages of Hobyo and Harardhere in the central area of Somalia. According to some reports, senior officials in Puntland are believed to be abetting piracy networks.

Somali piracy rose to global prominence with an increase in attacks during 2008 (111 attacked and 47 hijacked), record ransom payments (a reported $3.2 million was paid for the release of the *MV Faina*), and the deployment of over 30 naval vessels from over a dozen nations in the Gulf of Aden and the Indian Ocean. It is noteworthy that actual and attempted hijackings rose significantly in spite of the deployment of a multi-nation armada in late 2008. Records indicate that hijackings between January and end-of-May 2009 surpassed the total for 2008; also, attacks during the first quarter of 2009 were ten times higher than the same period in 2008. Somali piracy affects vessels from various parts of the world and impacts global trade via its effects on the global shipping industry (an estimated $500 million in 2008).

Who Are the Pirates?

Somali pirates are generally young (late teens to early 30s) and are drawn from the vast number of poorly educated, unemployed and disaffected men. They are usually armed with automatic rifles (AK-47), rocket-propelled grenades and an assortment of light weapons. Three broad categories of pirates could be identified: battle-hardened clan-based militia, youth looking for quick money to finance plans (like marriage or emigration) and fishermen who are forcibly recruited for their navigational skills.

Pirates typically operate in gangs of four to six people, and are organized and provided with boats, weapons and supplies by a handful of "pirate bosses." Their financiers, based further inland, do not engage in piracy directly. They invest in the piracy enterprise in the expectation of sharing in any ransom that is generated. The pirate bosses are critical to the perpetuation of Somalia's major piracy networks.

As piracy . . . became increasingly common, ships began to steer well clear of the Somali coast. This has required the pirates to operate further out to sea.

GlobalSecurity.com lists four networks, while experts at an international expert group meeting which met in Kenya in November 2008 listed five. Each network is comprised of dozens of armed militia, a few conscripted fishermen and hundreds of unemployed young men loosely organized in gangs.

Somali piracy is brazen, but remains a relatively low-tech affair. Pirates utilize small skiffs which can travel up to 30 knots. Coordinated attacks involving three to five of these boats are used in tandem to swarm targeted vessels until the pirates can board a ship with grappling hooks and ladders.

Multiple skiffs distract and unsettle the crew on the targeted vessel until one gang is able to board, followed by the others. Ships that get hijacked are usually slow vessels (traveling 15 knots or less), with low sides (or at least sitting low in the water).

As piracy in the Indian Ocean became increasingly common, ships began to steer well clear of the Somali coast. This has required the pirates to operate further out to sea. To do so, they have developed a "mothership" strategy of seizing medium-size fishing trawlers, holding their crew captive, and using the trawler to lay in wait for larger, more lucrative target vessels to pass. If no suitable targets are found in the short-term, pirates may return to shore in northern Somalia or possibly eastern Yemen in order to refuel and re-supply, before setting out to sea once more.

Hijacked vessels tend to have limited crews or lack an effective look-out for pirates that would enable them to take evasive measures. They also generally lack non-lethal protective measures such as water cannons or acoustical devices to ward off attacks. Targets vary and have included: oil tankers like the *Sirius Star*, cargo vessels like *MV Faina*; fishing vessels like *Playa de Bakio*; relief cargo ships like the *Maersk Alabama*; luxury yachts like *Le Ponant*; and cruise ships like the *Seaborn Spirit*.

Although most pirate gangs seek targets of opportunity, successful gangs are believed to receive ship information . . . from port or government officials.

The Pirate Business Model

Piracy operations unfold in seven phases: reconnaissance and information gathering; coordinated pursuit; boarding and takeover; steaming to safe area; negotiations; ransom payment; and disembarkation and safe passage.

Although most pirate gangs seek targets of opportunity, successful gangs are believed to receive ship information (ship routing, capacity, cargo, crew and defenses) from port or government officials. Armed with this information, they lie in wait to execute a coordinated attack. This reconnaissance and information gathering phase helps reduce operating costs and focus the efforts of the pirate gangs. Coordinated attacks (described above) usually result in boarding and takeover. According to most reports, a pirate attack takes approximately fifteen minutes to complete. Once a ship is commandeered by the gang(s), the crew is forced to steer towards a favored pirate mooring, usually off villages such as Garad, Eyl, Hobyo or Harardhere, in northeast or central Somalia. This reduces the likelihood of rescue and facilitates the provision of supplies for the pirates and their captives during the negotiation process—which could last for days or months.

Most ransoms are delivered directly to the hijacked ships either by boats hired by private security companies contracted by shipping agents and their insurance companies or, more recently, via drops to hijacked vessels from specially equipped light aircraft. Estimates of annual ransom paid to Somali pirate networks in 2008 vary from $50 million to $130 million. Hijacked vessels are released and granted safe passage after the ransom is paid. The actual and perceived success of piracy has led to a proliferation of recruits and an ever-increasing number of pirate gangs. . . .

According to reports from captured pirates, they traditionally divide some 30 percent of the ransom payment equally among themselves. This provides them with two to three times the income of the average worker. According to a United Nations report, piracy receipts in Puntland are three times the region's income. These funds help sustain officials who provide assistance to the pirates. This guarantees the continued flow of intelligence and support. The apparent profitability of the business model and the ease of entry from the large pool of unemployed Somalis have swollen the ranks of the pirates.

Somali Pirates Are Becoming More Sophisticated and Daring in Their Attacks

Lauren Ploch, Christopher M. Blanchard, Ronald O'Rourke, R. Chuck Mason, and Rawle O. King

Lauren Ploch, Christopher M. Blanchard, Ronald O'Rourke, R. Chuck Mason, and Rawle O. King are analysts at the Congressional Research Service, a public policy research arm of the United States Congress.

Piracy has reemerged as a global security threat, most recently in the waters off the Horn of Africa, but also in West Africa, the waters off India, the South China Sea and the Strait of Malacca [Indonesia], and the Caribbean. Pirates tend to operate in regions with large coastal areas, high levels of commercial activity, small national naval forces, and weak regional security cooperation mechanisms. These characteristics facilitate other maritime security threats, including maritime terrorism, weapons and narcotics trafficking, illegal fishing and dumping, and human smuggling operations.

A Growing Problem

Worldwide rates of piracy began to increase in the early 1990s, peaking at roughly 350 to 450 reported attacks per year during the period 2000–2004, then declining by almost half by 2005. In 2007, almost half of the world's reported pirate attacks took place in African waters, mainly near Nigeria and Somalia. The number of attacks in Somali waters doubled in 2008, accounting for an estimated 40% of the 293 pirate attacks reported worldwide. The recent increase in pirate attacks

Lauren Ploch, Christopher M. Blanchard, Ronald O'Rourke, R. Chuck Mason, and Rawle O. King, "Piracy Off the Horn of Africa," *Congressional Research Service*, April 19, 2010, pp. 5–13. http://assets.opencrs.com. Copyright © 2010 by Congressional Research Service. All rights reserved. Reproduced by permission.

off Somalia has caused the total number of worldwide pirate attacks to return to the levels of 2000–2004: of the 406 worldwide attacks in 2009, 217 of them occurred off the coast of Somalia. Moreover, high-profile attacks on high value vessels in the Gulf of Aden and the west Indian Ocean have brought renewed international attention to the problem of piracy in waters off the Horn of Africa.

The U.S. National Maritime Security Strategy, issued in 2005, stated that the "safety and economic security of the United States depends upon the secure use of the world's oceans," and identified "well organized and well equipped" pirates and criminals as threats to international maritime security. The bombing of the *U.S.S. Cole* in 2000 in the Yemeni harbor of Aden and the bombing of the French oil tanker *MV Limburg* in 2002 illustrated the threat of potential maritime terrorism in the region. The United States, working with its international partners, established a combined naval task force to meet the terrorism threat (Combined Task Force 150), and increased bilateral military and security assistance to regional navies. However, prior to the establishment in January 2009 of the new Combined Task Force 151 (see "Combined Task Force 151" below), the United States had not assigned any naval assets the sole task of performing anti-piracy operations in the Horn of Africa region.

Similarly, until 2008, the international community did not respond to the threat of piracy in the waters off of Somalia in a coordinated, dedicated manner. In December 2008, the European Union launched EU NAVFOR Operation ATALANTA, representing the first naval operation under the framework of the European Security and Defense Policy (ESDP). Similarly, NATO [North Atlantic Treaty Organization] has launched a dedicated anti-piracy mission, Operation Ocean Shield, and other navies have deployed ships to provide security for vessels bearing their flags. The development of a collaborative regional response in East Africa in 2009 mirrored regional reactions to the threat of piracy in the Strait of Malacca between Malaysia, Singapore and Indonesia, which are credited with having drastically reduced the instance of piracy in Southeast Asia since 2005. Eradicating piracy in the Horn of Africa region may prove to be a more daunting task. The vast areas of the western Indian Ocean and the Gulf of Aden where the pirates operate are remote, Somalia remains largely ungoverned, and regional states have relatively weak naval capabilities. . . .

The number of attacks in Somali waters doubled in 2008, . . . [and] of the 406 worldwide attacks in 2009, 217 of them occurred off the coast of Somalia.

A Profile of the Pirates

Several groups of pirates currently operate in Somali waters, according to reports from the United Nations [UN] Secretary General, an experts group convened by the Secretary General's Special Representative for Somalia in November 2008, and the U.N. Monitoring Group on Somalia established pursuant to Security Council resolution 1853 (2008). Organized predominantly along clan lines and based in distinct, remote port towns, the groups have varying capabilities and patterns of operation, making generalized responses more difficult. The two primary groups identified by the U.N. Monitoring Group in its March 2010 report are a pirate network based in the Mudug region district of Harardera (Xarardheere) and two pirate networks based in the Puntland region district of Eyl and Garad. The Secretary General and the Special Representative's experts group also report that smaller pirate groups also operate from the Somali ports of Bosaso, Qandala, Caluula, Bargaal, Hobyo, and Mogadishu. The Secretary General has warned that some of the pirate groups "now rival established Somali authorities in terms of their military capabilities and resource bases." Pirate groups have operated from many of these remote communities, each heavily dependent on fishing, since the early 1990s.

Several of the pirate groups have adopted names to suggest that they are acting in a maritime security capacity, and some reports suggest that some of the pirates may have previously received training by Somalia's former navy and by foreign security firms and been given semi-official status to intercept foreign fishing vessels and extract fines. Today, the pirates are collectively referred to by Somalis as *burcad badeed* (sea bandits). Nevertheless, piracy appears to have become an attractive pursuit for young men, creating potential legal complexities for regional and international governments seeking to try young pirate suspects for alleged crimes.

The northern semi-autonomous region of Puntland appears to be home to the most active and capable pirate networks, and some regional and local government officials there are alleged to have facilitated and profited from piracy in spite of some limited recent efforts by regional leaders to crack down on piracy-related corruption. In March 2010, the U.N. Monitoring Group on Somalia reported that key leaders in the Puntland administration "have received proceeds from piracy and or kidnapping," and, that "in some cases the Puntland authorities have extended protection to pirate militias." Puntland authorities protested the report's conclusions and characterized them as politically motivated. In August 2009, the TFG [transitional federal government of Somalia] and the Puntland authorities agreed to a joint program for anti-piracy cooperation, and, in November 2009, the Secretary General reported that local Puntland authorities "have succeeded in launching limited relevant activities to thwart, curb, or investigate piracy." Puntland's regional authorities have developed a basic coast guard, but accounts suggest that the equipment and capabilities of this small force remain very limited.

The Motives for Piracy

According to the final report of the experts group convened in November 2008 by U.N. Special Representative to Somalia Ahmedou Ould-Abdallah, "poverty, lack of employment, environmental hardship, pitifully low incomes, reduction of pastoralist [shepherding] and maritime resources due to drought and illegal fishing and a volatile security and political situation all contribute to the rise and continuance of piracy in Somalia." While the profitability of piracy appears to be the primary motivating factor for most pirates, other observers argue that since conditions in Somalia make survival difficult for many and prosperity elusive for most, the relative risk of engagement in piracy seems diminished.

The use of force by international naval patrols . . . has raised the prospect that revenge may become a motivating factor for pirates whose associates are killed or captured.

Somali pirates interviewed by international media sources frequently link their piracy activities to trends such as illegal fishing and dumping in Somali waters that have emerged as the country has lost its ability to patrol its waters over time. While these explanations may mask the opportunistic piracy of some, reports suggest that illegal fishing and dumping have disrupted Somalia's coastal economy. For example, a July 2005 report from the United Kingdom Department for International Development (DFID) estimated that Somalis lost $100 million to illegal tuna and shrimp fishing in the country's exclusive economic zone in 2003–2004.

The international Contact Group on Piracy off the Coast of Somalia (CGPCS) stated at its inaugural meeting that "piracy is symptomatic of the overall situation in Somalia including the prevalence of illegal fishing and toxic waste dumping off the coast of Somalia, which adversely affects the Somali economy and marine environment." The CGPCS also reaffirmed "its respect for Somalia's sovereignty, territorial integrity, and sovereign rights over natural resources" and underscored that the group's participants "ensure that their flagged vessels respect these rights."

Paradoxically, the regional fishing industry reportedly has been damaged significantly by the threat of piracy. According to some reports, tuna catches in the Indian Ocean fell 30% in 2008, in part because of fishing vessels' fears of piracy. This has had a major impact on countries like the Seychelles, which rely on the fishing industry for up to 40% of their earnings.

The use of force by international naval patrols to apprehend or kill pirate suspects has raised the prospect that revenge may become a motivating factor for pirates whose associates are killed or captured. The April 14, 2009, attack on the U.S.-flagged *MV Liberty Sun* allegedly was carried out with the intention of damaging or sinking the ship and injuring or killing its crew in retaliation for the deaths of three Somali pirates during U.S. military efforts to secure the release of the detained captain of the *MV Maersk Alabama* days earlier. According to the U.S. Office of Naval Intelligence (ONI), as of December 30, 2009, the number of vessels fired upon by Somali pirates in 2009 (127) was triple the number fired upon during 2008 (42).

When ships operating [off the Somalian coast] shifted further out to sea, Somali pirates shifted their focus to the Gulf of Aden, where there is a concentration of merchant ships.

Pirate Tactics and Demands

As noted above, some Somali pirate groups have developed sophisticated operational capabilities and have acquired weaponry, equipment, and funds that make them on par with or more effective than the local forces arrayed against them. The typical Somali pirate team is equipped with a variety of small arms, including AK-47 rifles and rocket propelled grenade (RPG) launchers. Many pirate teams use fishing skiffs powered with large outboard motors to give chase to larger, but slower moving tankers, cargo ships, yachts, cruise ships, barges, and tug boats. Local Somali fishermen reportedly are forced to support pirate activities in some cases, while in other cases, coastal Somalis lend their fishing boats, equipment, and navigational expertise to teams of would-be pirates from inland communities.

Somali pirates initially focused on attacking ships in the western Indian Ocean, off Somalia's eastern coast. When ships operating on that route shifted further out to sea, Somali pirates shifted their focus to the Gulf of Aden, where there is a concentration of merchant ships (an estimated 33,000 per year) operating in a more constrained waterway that is relatively close to Somalia's northern shore. Most recently, now that international naval forces are patrolling the Gulf of Aden with some effectiveness, Somali pirates have shifted some of their focus back to the Indian Ocean, and are now able to operate hundreds of nautical miles from the Somali coastline, often with the support of so-called 'mother ships.' These 'mother ships' are larger fishing vessels often acquired or commandeered by acts of piracy, and tend to operate out of the Somali ports of Bosaso and Mogadishu and the Yemeni ports of Al Mukalla and Ash Shihr.

U.S. and international officials suspect that in some cases, Somali businessmen and international support networks provide pirate groups with financing and supplies in return for shares of ransom payments that are also distributed among pirates themselves. The IMB [International Maritime Bureau] has disputed claims that pirates receive intelligence support in order to target specific vessels, arguing that "the suggestion that vessels are targeted in advance using shore based intelligence is spurious. . . . Further, there is no information in the public domain that would enable pirates to precisely locate a targeted vessel at sea and then to mount a successful attack off the Horn of Africa." In March 2010, the U.S. Office of Naval Intelligence (ONI) reported that "vessels attacked off Somalia are randomly selected and not specifically targeted for any reason other than how easily the vessel can be boarded. Pirates simply patrol an area, wait for a target of opportunity, and attempt to board." The pirates refuel and purchase logistical supplies like fuel and engine parts in Yemen, according to U.S. naval officials. According to the NATO Shipping Center, Somali pirates returning from raids in the Gulf of Aden often stop at the port of Caluula on the northeast tip of Somalia before proceeding to their safe havens on the Indian Ocean coast.

One of the unique characteristics of Somali piracy has been the taking of hostages for ransom. In this sense, piracy off Somalia can be viewed as a form of maritime kidnapping. Unlike pirate attacks in the Strait of Malacca or Nigeria, where ships are boarded either to take the vessel or its contents, pirates off the Horn of Africa routinely take the target vessel's crew hostage in return for ransom payments. This approach to piracy is possible because the pirates have a sanctuary on land in Somalia and in its territorial waters from which they can launch pirate attacks and conduct ransom negotiations. Pirates in other parts of the world are less likely to have such sanctuaries. This has presented maritime security forces with significant challenges to traditional engagement strategies and tactics.

According to reports, most vessels under attack have less than 15 to 30 minutes between the first sighting of the pirates and their boarding of the ship and taking of hostages. If a naval ship cannot arrive on scene within those 15 to 30 minutes, it will likely arrive too late to prevent the ship's capture. Naval combatant ships generally can steam at speeds of up to 30 knots (speeds of 20+ knots might be more likely), so unless a naval ship happens to be a few miles away when a commercial ship comes under attack, it won't arrive until after the 15- to 30-minute window has come and gone. The large area of water to be patrolled and the relatively small number of naval ships available means that the closest naval ship is often far too distant to arrive within that timeframe.

One of the unique characteristics of Somali piracy has been the taking of hostages for ransom.

While pirate attacks may involve violence and the use of weaponry, most Somali pirate groups have not shown a willingness to wantonly harm captives taken in the course of their raids. Pirates in other parts of the world who engage in these types of attacks might be more likely to kill or seriously wound merchant ship crew members, since extracting ransom payments is not their objective. Negotiations for ransom involve the use of satellite telephones, third-party intermediaries in Somalia and abroad, and public relations efforts to influence interaction with property owners and foreign officials. Most navies have avoided rescue operations that could endanger the lives of hostages, preferring instead to engage in hostage negotiations or wait for shipping companies to negotiate ransom. According to reports, a rescue operation by French naval forces, designed to free a family held hostage onboard a small sailboat off the Somali coast, resulted in the death of the vessel's owner, a French citizen, during an exchange of fire between the pirates and naval personnel.

Prior to the U.S. military resolution of the *MV Maersk Alabama* seizure and other French military operations, the most sensational cases of piracy to date had been resolved through the payment of large sums of money to different pirate syndicates. The Ukrainian ship *MV Faina* was released for a reported $3.2 million ransom in February 2009 after being held for nearly 6 months by pirates based in Harardera (Xarardheere). The seizure of the ship, carrying T-72 tanks and a significant amount of ammunition and small arms, led several governments, including the United States, to dispatch naval forces to the region to monitor the ship and its cargo. The Saudi oil supertanker *MV Sirius Star* was released for a reported $3 million ransom to Eyl-based pirates in January 2009 following its seizure in November 2008. Similarly, reports suggested Somali pirates received a $4 million ransom in December 2009 to release the Chinese bulk coal carrier *MV De Xin Hai.*

Some pirates have invested ransom earnings in sophisticated weaponry and have fortified their operating bases.

The hijacking of the *MV Sirius Star, MV De Xin Hai, MV Maran Centaurus,* and the April 2010 hijacking of the *MT Sambo Dream* illustrate the threat piracy can pose to international energy supplies as well as the capabilities of some Somali pirates to operate far out to sea against large vessels. Ransom payments are considered to be problematic by some observers because they encourage pirates to continue their attacks with the expectation that insurance and shipping companies will decide that ransoms are cost effective relative to the insured values of personnel and cargo.

The use of force by international naval forces to apprehend pirates and to free hostages in 2009 has raised the prospect of an escalation in the pirates' use of force. As noted above, pirate leaders vowed to retaliate for the deaths of some of their operatives at the hands of U.S. and other international naval forces. However, to date few hostages have been harmed in pirate attacks. Nonetheless, the use of force against suspected pirate vessels also may be problematic because of the difficulty inherent in distinguishing a pirate mother ship from a legitimate commercial ship. According to reports, in November 2008, a ship from the Indian navy attacked what it thought was a pirate mother ship, only to discover, after the attack was conducted, that the targeted ship was an innocent Thai commercial trawler.

The effective use of force against pirate strongholds in coastal towns would likely require significant military planning and the investment of considerable resources in order to avoid or minimize civilian casualties. The number of naval ships that would be needed to completely halt piracy in the Gulf of Aden and the waters of Somalia's eastern coast is probably much larger than the force that has been operating there recently, approximately 40 combatant ships as of early 2010. According to some estimates, as many as 60 might be required to fully suppress piracy in the Gulf of Aden alone. The adjoining area of concern in the Indian Ocean off Somalia's eastern coast, which has been measured at more than 1 million square miles, is much larger than the Gulf of Aden, so completely halting piracy in that area would likely also require an even larger number of ships.

Reports suggest that some pirates have invested ransom earnings in sophisticated weaponry and have fortified their operating bases against local authorities and potential international intervention. Some observers warn that international military operations to combat pirates ashore with force could undermine political reconciliation efforts aimed at reestablishing national governance in Somalia.

Somali Pirates Raise Ransom Stakes

Colin Freeman

Colin Freeman is the chief foreign correspondent for the British newspaper the Sunday Telegraph *and is author of the 2011 book* Kidnapped: Life as a Hostage on Somalia's Pirate Coast.

Three months after he swapped them for a $5.4 million ransom, Budiga the Pirate still dances a wicked jig in the dreams of the crew of the *Marida Marguerite*. On some occasions, sailor Sandeep Dangwal remembers the day Budiga trussed him up on deck and tortured him. On others, he recalls the day Budiga stripped the ship's captain naked and forced him into the deep freeze, or the time a fellow crewman was left to hang by his wrists from a 40-foot mast.

"Budiga was the nastiest pirate devil ever," said Mr Dangwal, 26, who spent eight months as a hostage. "I still have bad dreams about that bastard now, and whenever I hear about a new ship being hijacked it upsets me. I hate to think that other people might suffer what I suffered."

Talking last week from his home outside Delhi, Mr Dangwal is the first sailor to speak out about a sinister new trend in Somalia's piracy epidemic, in which the modern-day buccaneers are turning to the kind of brutality more associated with their medieval predecessors.

While the pirate victims of yesteryear might fear the cat o'nine tails or walking the plank, today they risk punishments such as being "cooled" in a ship's walk-in freezer, "cooked" on a hot metal shipdeck in the midday sun, or forced to phone a distraught relative while a pirate fires a Kalashnikov in close earshot.

Colin Freeman, "Somali Pirates Raise Ransom Stakes," *The Daily Telegraph*, April 10, 2011. www.telegraph.co.uk. Copyright © 2011 by *The Daily Telegraph*. All rights reserved. Reproduced by permission.

Previously known for treating hostages relatively well, the pirate gangs have adopted a new ruthlessness to pressure ship owners into paying ever higher ransoms, which already total hundreds of millions of dollars every year.

[Pirate victims] risk punishments such as being "cooled" in a ship's walk-in freezer, [or] "cooked" on a hot metal shipdeck in the midday sun.

Coupled with figures which show that the number of piracy attacks is still increasing, the trend has prompted a new level of alarm through the international maritime world. Leading figures in the British shipping industry have told *The Sunday Telegraph* that Western naval forces must now take far tougher action to prevent the problem "spiralling out of control".

At the same time, maritime trade unions have warned that their members may soon refuse to sail through the pirate "high risk" area—which now covers much of the western Indian Ocean. Such a move would paralyse the key global shipping route through the Suez Canal, and also threaten oil supplies from the Persian Gulf.

"It's not just about the seafarers who are unlucky enough to be hijacked, it is stressful for all sailors who transit through the area, who now face four or five days in fear of their lives," said Jon Whitlow, of the International Transport Workers' Federation. "Who would put up with that in any other line of work?"

Uppermost in the unions' minds is the fate of ships like the *Marida Marguerite*, a 13,000 tonne chemical container vessel that was taken last May. For the first three months, the 22 crew were treated humanely, but as ransom talks dragged on, the pirates' patience frayed.

"They took me on deck one day and tied my hands and my legs behind my back for two hours, and also tightened a cable around my genitals," said Mr Dangwal, an engine technician. "When I screamed, they tightened it more."

Others suffered even more. The ship's captain was put naked into the vessel's freezer with his underwear filled with ice, spending half an hour in temperatures of minus 17C. When the chief engineer got the same treatment, and tried running around to keep warm, the pirates hung him from the freezer's meathook. The sailor who was suspended by his wrists from the mast, meanwhile, passed out after two hours.

"There was a period when none of us thought we'd come out alive," said sailor Dipendra Singh Rathore, 22, a devout Hindu, who was so distraught that at one point he gave up praying. "I was not personally beaten much, but hearing what was happening to the others was bad enough."

Previously known for treating hostages relatively well, the pirate gangs have adopted a new ruthlessness to pressure ship owners into paying ever higher ransoms.

According to Major General Buster Howes, the British commander of the European Union Naval Force, there are now "regular manifestations of systematic torture" by pirate gangs. There has even been one incident of "keelhauling", a 15th-century pirate practice in which sailors are thrown over one side of a ship and dragged by a rope under the keel to the other.

"It is barbaric," said Bill Box, of Intertanko, the international association of independent tanker owners. "If they pull the sailor too quick, he will be ripped apart by the barnacles on the ship's underside, and if they pull him too slowly, he may drown."

While still confined to a minority of hijack cases, such brutality runs counter to the pirates' carefully-cultivated image as African "Robin Hoods". Until now, they have prided themselves on using only the minimum force necessary, claiming merely to be "taxing" passing vessels in revenge for foreign poaching of their fish stocks.

One theory is that as foreign navies have tried to crack down on the problem, the ex-fishermen who originally dominated the piracy game have been replaced by hardened militiamen, who are also more likely to stand their ground when confronted. Seven hostages have died this year in stand-offs with the 25-odd foreign warships patrolling the region, including four American yachters on the *SV Quest* in February.

Another evolution in pirate tactics is the use of "mother ships"—hijacked vessels which allow them to range for hundreds of miles, and which serve as floating jails for hostages.

As foreign navies have tried to crack down on the problem, the ex-fishermen who originally dominated the piracy game have been replaced by hardened militiamen.

Two weeks ago, the Indian Navy launched an attack on another mother ship, a Mozambican trawler called the Vega 5, arresting some 61 pirates and rescuing 13 hijacked crew members. But up to a dozen others still remain operational, despite the multi-national fleet knowing where they are. European naval commanders insist that attacking them carries too much risk of hostages getting killed, however, such is the threat that the shipping industry says only a "military solution" is now practical.

"The mother ships represent an industrialisation of piracy, and we have to find a way of breaking the cycle," said Gavin Simmonds, head of international policy at the British Chamber of Shipping.

"The military has got to be more robust, as the consequences of leaving the situation as it is are greater than those of using greater force."

Hijacking figures appear to back the view that the anti-piracy fleet is having little effect. Last year saw a record 1,016 crew members taken hostage, compared with 867 in 2009 and 815 in 2008, according to the International Maritime Bureau.

"The situation has not improved," said Captain Pottengal Mukundan, director of the bureau's piracy reporting centre. "Ransom demands are higher, and they are keeping ships for longer—some have been held for more than a year."

Some now go as far as to back a "shoot on sight" policy. Jacob Stolt-Nielsen, a Norwegian shipping magnate, said earlier this year that history proved it to be the only effective way to police areas as large as oceans. "I'm just telling it like it is," he said. "The way to solve the pirate problem is to sink the pirates and their ships."

However, any more "robust" approach would involve Western navies reassessing their current rules of engagement, which generally allow lethal force only when they are directly engaged in acts piracy, and which place some emphasis on pirates' human rights

Not surprisingly, that is a consideration that Mr Dangwal has little time for. Anything that stops Budiga claiming more victims is justified, he says. "These aren't pirates, they are terrorists. There should be no mercy."

Somali Piracy Is Threatening Global Shipping and Manufacturing

Stephanie Nall

Stephanie Nall is a writer and editor from the Los Angeles area.

The world's largest container line says piracy is increasing its insurance costs and forcing it to pass those costs along to customers in the form of "piracy surcharges." But for cargo owners and vessel operators alike, the costs of armed, and sometimes deadly, attacks go beyond insurance to time, new expenses and business disruptions.

Increased Insurance Costs

Maersk Line is increasing the amount it charges customers whose cargo goes into or out of East African ports by $50 or $100 per container. For cargo on vessels that merely travel through the Gulf of Aden to another destination, Maersk says new "war risk charges" will be $25 for each 20-foot container and $50 for each 40-foot container. The Danish carrier said the increase is needed to offset additional insurance costs it faces because of the escalating piracy problem in the region.

Increasing numbers of pirate hijackings and hijack attempts are driving up insurance premiums in ways that are hard to calculate across the board. The Congressional Research Service says in a recent study that one group of London insurance brokers and underwriters estimates extra premiums at $10,000 to $20,000 per trip through the Gulf of Aden.

Richard Manson, spokesman for the Allianz Group's corporate and specialty lines of insurance, said the effects of the

Stephanie Nall, "The Costs of Piracy Are Passed Along," America.gov, June 1, 2009. Copyright © 2009 by US Department of State, Bureau of International Information. All rights reserved. Reproduced by permission.

attacks vary too widely to give even a range for voyages into or through the Gulf of Aden. Some carriers and cargo owners fear that the increased insurance premiums will translate into higher costs for all vessels, no matter what trade route they travel, but that is not yet happening. "Across the board, we aren't seeing increases," said Manson, whose group insures clients with different risk levels, different size vessels and different types of cargo and routes.

The most discernible industry trend is one of moving the piracy-benefits coverage for commercial ships from general liability policies, which include hull insurance, to war policies, Manson said.

Increasing numbers of pirate hijackings and hijack attempts are driving up insurance premiums.

Compared to the standard war risk insurance rate, premiums being levied for voyages across the Gulf of Aden are about five times higher, according to Bob DeMotta, managing director of the marine practice group for Aon Risk Services, an insurance broker.

The rates are a percentage of the insured value. For example, a vessel insured for $50 million would have a standard annual war risk insurance of about $10,000. The additional war risk premium for transit across the Gulf of Aden would be $62,500 per voyage. DeMotta said rates are higher now, not only for war risk insurance, but also for primary hull and liability insurance.

Some insurance carriers offer separate kidnap and ransom policies (pirates were paid an estimated $30 million in ransoms in 2008), but most companies won't discuss it publicly. "That is so sensitive," Manson said. "Lives are at stake. We won't do anything to signal to the hijackers one way or the other."

Low Risk of Attack

Piracy got a jolt of attention in the United States in April [2009], when pirates seized the *Maersk Alabama*, a container vessel operated by Maersk Line Ltd., the U.S.-flag subsidiary of Maersk Line.

Yet the overall risk of attack, even off the Somali coast, is relatively low, according to a spokesman for Maersk Line Ltd. "There are 22,000 to 30,000 vessels that transit the Gulf of Aden each year," said Kevin Speers. "With several dozen ships seized each year and about 100 vessels fired on, that's a 0.167 percent chance that a vessel will be involved [in a piracy incident]. Bad weather presents a larger risk, and that's the sort of thing insurance companies look at."

The insurance increases are so substantial that some carriers are considering rerouting their vessels and sailing around the Cape of Good Hope instead of going through the Suez Canal.

The Long Way

But the head of a freight forwarder with business around Africa said piracy is causing severe harm to transportation now. "We are one of the lucky ones and thus far have not been directly caught in the melee," said Peter Schauer, chief executive of Orion Marine. "It's not just the value of the ship or cargo [at risk], but there is danger for personnel. All of that directly translates into higher costs. The insurance increases are so substantial that some carriers are considering rerouting their vessels and sailing around the Cape of Good Hope instead of going through the Suez Canal."

For economically pressed carriers, the long way around has two advantages: avoiding higher insurance rates and avoiding the Suez Canal toll. The average toll for container vessels using the canal is $600,000. With fuel costs down and hundreds of surplus vessels laid up around the globe, the slower route has economic allure for the shipping industry.

Costs to Manufacturers

But rerouting vessels and other delays—for example, those caused by the need to join a military convoy—add to supply chain disruptions, which are costing manufacturers. Robert Mawanda, spokesman for the Uganda Manufacturers Association, said delays can cause factory shutdowns if parts or raw materials don't arrive on time. And if carriers avoid certain ports (Mogadishu, Somalia, or Mombasa, Kenya) to give wide berth to pirates, it may force companies to elect an even longer and more expensive alternative: ground transportation.

Some manufacturers in Uganda have resorted to paying air freight charges for critical parts, even though it might be more than 10 times as expensive, Mawanda said. With the global economic slowdown and a weak Ugandan shilling, any pirate-related disruption of the supply chain increases production costs and presents "a difficult and complex problem for our manufacturers," he said.

That is why, he said, despite the fact that most association members "never bothered with cargo insurance before, now they can't afford to forego the expense."

Somalia's Piracy Problem Affects All Nations

Claude Berube

Claude Berube, a reserve officer in the US Navy, is a writer, author, and instructor in the political science department at the US Naval Academy.

Humor has its place, but today's piracy is no laughing matter. Piracy permeates our cultural ethos—it's in children's stories and movies both tragic and comical. In recent months, as pirates off Somalia have proliferated and widened the scope of their capability, newspapers, television newscasts, and bloggers have invariably invoked the terms "arrghh," "avast," and "Pirates of the Caribbean." One essay casually suggested building a Jack Sparrow (referring to the lead character in the movie "Pirates of the Caribbean") wing at Guantánamo [Bay, a US military prison in Cuba].

But maritime piracy involves criminal elements using force against innocent prey whose only interest is safe passage. Little more, little less. The problem of piracy is as ancient as when mankind first traversed open waters. [Greek historian] Thucydides notes in his history of the Peloponnesian War that piracy was rampant until [King] Minos built a navy to secure the sea lanes. We've mostly endured it until it reached a certain threshold, such as when the US finally sent ships to address the threat to legitimate commerce during the Barbary war in the early 1800s. But recent Somali piracy has caused the international community to take notice. And for good reason.

Claude Berube, "Somalia's Piracy Problem Is Everyone's Problem," *Christian Science Monitor*, December 8, 2008. www.csmonitor.com. Copyright © 2008 by *Christian Science Monitor*. All rights reserved. Reproduced by permission.

High Stakes Piracy

Pirates have increased the stakes. No longer are just yachts, fishing boats, and small freighters at risk; now there are attacks on cruise ships (the *Nautica*), military cargo (the freighter *Faina*), a chemical tanker (the *Biscaglia*), and an oil carrier. The *Sirius Star*, hijacked last month [November 2008], contains a reported two million barrels of crude oil. By comparison, the *Exxon Valdez*, which accidentally grounded in Prince William Sound nearly 20 years ago, could hold 1.2 million barrels and spilled one-third of that, resulting in one of the top environmental disasters.

There is some precedent for using oil as a weapon—at the start of the Gulf War in 1991, [Iraqi dictator] Saddam Hussein ordered an estimated 11 million barrels of crude oil to be poured into the Gulf. What ecological damage could a criminal or terrorist organization effect with such a ship?

> *Pirates have increased the stakes.... Now there are attacks on cruise ships ..., military cargo ..., a chemical tanker ..., and an oil carrier.*

Last month, the Office of the Director of National Intelligence released its report, "Global Trends 2025—a Transformed World," which suggested, in part, that "some states might wither away as governments fail to provide security and other basic needs." While not all potential failed states are located in proximity to major shipping lanes, as Somalia is with the Gulf of Aden, port facilities or oil and gas fields might be at risk to future stateless areas and/or nonstate actors.

Piracy Hurts Everyone

With the exception of private pleasure craft attacked on occasion in the Caribbean, piracy no longer occurs around North America. In distant waters, few US built, flagged, or manned commercial ships ply their trade; therefore few US ships are affected. But while piracy may not present an immediate or direct threat to US national security interests, its consequences can affect everyone.

Insurance rates for ships transiting the Gulf of Aden are increasing 10-fold. The risk to personnel and cargo if a ship is hijacked is escalating, and tens of millions of dollars have already been paid out in ransom to pirates this year [2008].

Piracy can affect local economies, too. Egypt, for example, earned $5 billion in the past year from ships transiting the Suez Canal. Some shipping companies have already begun diverting their ships around the Horn of Africa, further increasing their costs due to a longer transit and reducing revenue for Egypt. But as the hijacking of the *Sirius Star* far from the Gulf of Aden demonstrated, even the longer transit may not be as safe now.

While piracy may not present an immediate or direct threat to US national security interests, its consequences can affect everyone.

Although speculation has been raised about ties between terrorist organizations and pirates, experts agree that it is just that—speculation. That said, an act of piracy may have occurred last week [in December 2008] before the terrorist attacks in Mumbai (formerly Bombay) when a Pakistani fishing vessel, the *Kuber*, was allegedly hijacked by the terrorists, its crew killed, and the boat used to convey the attackers to India.

The issue is not whether piracy is tied to terrorism, but rather how terrorists or others might employ piratical tactics. If nonstate actors find the tactic is sound and the defense against it untenable, then it will be used to conduct similar or more spectacular operations. How would nonstate actors or other future belligerents interpret any success by the pirates? Absent an effective response to lawlessness, Somali piracy may be a prism to view potential copycat killers.

The United Nations Security Council is rightly addressing this 21st-century incarnation of the age-old maritime challenge. Resolutions have been passed and coalitions made, individual state forces are patrolling the region, enhanced private maritime security is being explored, and long-term methods of appropriate state-level response being debated. While all the answers may not be here yet, everyone is at least asking the questions.

CHAPTER 2

Is Piracy Connected to Terrorism?

Chapter Preface

Somalia is a coastal nation located on the Horn of Africa, a large peninsula on the eastern coast of the continent that juts out into the Indian Ocean to the east and the Gulf of Aden to the north. This is a vital sea route, especially for Persian Gulf oil—part of the Suez Canal shipping lane that connects the Mediterranean Sea with the world's oceans through the Red Sea. In recent years, this area has become known as pirate's alley because of the large numbers of attacks on merchant ships by Somali pirates. Most experts agree that the main cause of this growing piracy problem is that Somalia does not have a viable central government and thus is unable to police its own territorial waters or prosecute pirates who take refuge on land. Struggling in a state of civil war and clan conflict for decades, with no real economy, and facing a growing fundamentalist Islamic movement that some experts believe is connected to al Qaeda terrorists, Somalia ranks as one of the world's poorest and most dangerous nations.

Somalia's modern history began late in the nineteenth century, when European countries began trading in the area. Various parts of what is today the nation of Somalia came under British and Italian colonial rule as those nations established treaties with local rulers. After World War II, Italy and Britain gave up their control and the Italian and British parts of Somalia declared their independence; in 1960 they joined together to form the Somalia Republic. The following year, Somalia adopted a constitution that set up a parliamentary democracy. This experiment with democracy did not work, however, and Somalia soon entered a period of instability that continues to the present day.

The end of democracy for Somalia came in 1969, when a bloodless coup installed Major General Mohamed Siad Barre as president. Under Barre's rule, power rested with a Supreme

Revolutionary Council (SRC) headed by Barre himself, and this unelected, unaccountable government soon controlled all aspects of Somali life. For example, the Barre government regulated the flow of information, reduced political freedoms, redistributed rich farmland, and used military force and terror tactics to consolidate power and suppress opposition movements. Allied with the Soviet Union, Somalia also pursued an aggressive foreign policy that brought it into conflict with neighboring Ethiopia. Later, however, after relations with the Soviets deteriorated, Somalia realigned itself with the United States, receiving military training and aid.

By the 1980s, Barre's brutal reign had inspired the formation of numerous opposition groups, and Somalia erupted into civil war, with clans fighting against other clans for power. These insurgent movements caused great instability in the country as well as an economic crisis. Hundreds of thousands of Somalis fled from their homes to escape warfare and poverty, and the central government essentially collapsed. In January 1991, Barre was finally ousted and forced into exile.

The end of the Barre government, however, only brought more political chaos, death, and poverty to Somalia. Various groups fought for power, and more than a dozen peace conferences failed to mediate a peace among the warring factions. The country spiraled further and further into turmoil. In 1992, a United Nations effort led by the United States tried to deliver assistance to Somalis who were suffering from starvation and violence. However, after a 1993 incident known as Black Hawk Down, in which eighteen US servicemen were brutally killed by Somalis, the United States withdrew its forces.

Finally, in 2000, Ethiopia held a peace conference that resulted in the creation of the Transitional National Government (TNG), which was charged with governing Somalia for three years while parties tried to resolve their differences. In 2004, the TNG was replaced with the Transitional Federal

Government (TFG), the current governmental authority in Somalia. The TFG is working to form a new constitution and to hold elections to create a permanent government for Somalia. The TFG is supported by the United Nations, the United States, and the African Union (a group of African nations), but it has yet to consolidate power sufficiently to gain control of the country.

Recent years have seen the development of a strong fundamentalist Islamic movement, particularly in southern Somalia, that seeks to overthrow the TFG and establish an Islamic government. The strongest Islamic group is al-Shabaab, a group that the United States designates as a terrorist organization. Al-Shabaab's attacks limit the TFG's ability to provide public services and security and prevent the delivery of humanitarian aid to Somalis. Many terrorism experts worry if al-Shabaab succeeds in winning control of Somalia, the country may become the next haven for international terrorism. Some experts also warn that al-Shabaab is uniting forces with Somali pirates—a prospect that could lead to sea-based Islamic terrorism. The authors in this chapter explore this question of whether there is a connection between piracy and terrorism in Somalia.

The Somali Pirates Are Islamic Jihadists

Robert Spencer

Robert Spencer is an author and director of Jihad Watch, *a blog about Islamic theology and ideology.*

This week [April 15, 2009], we celebrate the Navy SEALs' rescue of American ship captain Richard Phillips. Their action, from the night airdrop that delivered them to the waiting warships to the split-second action in which three of the pirates were killed, was what we expect from our best special operations troops.

But while we praise their skill, let's not lose sight of who Phillips' captors were. His Somali pirate captors are Islamic jihadists, dedicated to the same goals as Osama bin Laden [leader of terrorist organization al Qaeda] and other jihadists around the world.

Piracy Funds Islamic Jihad

In August 2008, when the pirates became especially active off the Horn of Africa, Andrew Mwangura, head of the East African Seafarers' Assistance Programme, declared that Al-Shabaab, a group of jihadists in Somalia, use piracy to fund their jihad [holy war against non-Muslims]: "According to our information, the money they make from piracy and ransoms goes to support al-Shabaab activities onshore."

With ransoms for ships each bringing in at least $10,000 and some in multiple millions of dollars, and the pirates seizing ships at a furious rate (taking four in one forty-eight hour period last summer [2008]), piracy is a lucrative source of funding for the jihad. Journalist Stephen Brown noted in No-

Robert Spencer, "The Somali Pirates Are Jihadists," *Human Events*, April 15, 2009. www.HumanEvents.com. Copyright © 2009 by *Human Events*. All rights reserved. Reproduced by permission.

vember 2008 that "security experts fear the ransom money the pirates are receiving will allow them to buy better equipment and weapons for larger operations." And with astounding short-sightedness, European governments—with the notable exception of the French last week—have been paying these ransoms. In that light, the American refusal to do so, and the rescue of Phillips, is a welcome step in the right direction.

Al-Shabaab, a group of jihadists in Somalia, use piracy to fund their jihad.

But now it must be followed up properly, for al-Shabaab has numerous links to jihadist activity elsewhere. Al-Shabaab al-Mujahideen ("Jihadist Youth") is linked to al-Qaeda and advocates the strict application of Islamic law. It came to the fore in that troubled nation after the 2006 toppling by Ethiopian troops of the Islamic Courts Union government that ruled briefly in Mogadishu. And Mwangura notes that currently "the entire Somali coastline is now under control of the Islamists." Al-Shabaab now controls more of Somalia than the Islamic Courts Union did even at the height of its power, and its reach extends beyond Somalia. Some of the Somali immigrants who have mysteriously disappeared from the Minneapolis [Minnesota] area have been recruited for jihad by al-Shabaab, which has also attracted jihad fighters from around the world to join its efforts to take control in Somalia.

Not only are the Somali pirates Islamic jihadists, but their religious identity is much more important to them than being considered the sons and heirs of [historical pirates] Blackbeard and Captain Kidd. On Sunday, *Reuters* [news service] quoted one of the pirates saying, "We never kill people. We are Muslims. We are marines, coastguards—not pirates." Hostages have reported, however, that despite this pious disavowal, the pirates have threatened to kill them on more than one occasion. And the Navy SEALs only opened fire when it appeared [the pirates] were about to kill Capt. Phillips.

The Terror Threat

Counterterror analyst Olivier Guitta, exploring Al-Shabaab's connections with al-Qaeda, explained that the group "intends to take control of the Gulf of Aden and the southern entrance of the Red Sea." This creates an acute problem for [US president] Barack Obama. If al-Shabaab does gain control of Somalia, it will not only continue to threaten shipping but will almost certainly expand its jihadist reach beyond Somalia to destabilize the Horn of Africa and work with other jihadist elements in the area, just as it has attracted foreign jihadists to its own cause. What's more, the Somali jihad could come to the U.S. itself. In January [2008], *Newsweek* reported about al-Shabaab that "a jihadist group able to enlist U.S. nationals to fight abroad might also be able to persuade Somali-Americans to act as sleeper agents here in the United States." Al-Shabaab's al-Qaeda ties make it quite likely that such a thought has occurred to the group's leadership as well.

Accordingly, counterterror analysts and the mainstream media would do well to widen their narrow focus upon maritime piracy, and consider the role that this piracy is playing in the larger jihadist initiative. Unfortunately, with the Obama administration moving away even from the language of the "war on terror," it's unlikely that it will consider the implications of al-Shabaab's links with the global jihadist network.

In an April 2008 statement, al-Shabaab vowed to "throw the West into hell." Does Obama have the vision or the will to stand against this bloodlust before it grows even more powerful? And if so, what will he do?

Somali Pirates Are Financing Islamic Terrorists

Mohamed Ahmed and Abdi Sheikh

Mohamed Ahmed and Abdi Sheikh are contributors to Reuters, an international news agency based in London.

Somali Islamist rebels have demanded their fighters be allowed to board hijacked vessels anchored off the coastal town of Haradheere to monitor the payment and division of ransoms, escalating risks to hostages.

Islamists and Pirates

Islamists clamped down hard on piracy when they briefly ran much of Somalia in 2006, but with ransoms rising they now want a share of its earnings.

Hardline Islamist militants have surrounded the pirate base to pressure gang leaders and their investors into accepting the order, pirates and residents said on Monday [February 28, 2011], after a number tried to sail ships up the coast.

If rebels are allowed to board the vessels, hostages risk becoming stuck in the middle of dangerous rows or, worse, being kidnapped by [terrorist group] al Shabaab rebels, who claim ties with al Qaeda [terrorist organization responsible for September 11, 2001, attacks].

Shipowners fear any proven link between pirates and Islamist fighters will make it legally difficult to pay ransoms without running afoul of counter-terrorism legislation.

Pirates in Haradheere agreed last week to hand al Shabaab insurgents a 20 percent cut of ransoms but a deep distrust prevails between the two sides.

Mohamed Ahmed and Abdi Sheikh, "Somali Islamists Want to Do Ransom Deals on Board," Reuters, March 1, 2011. www.af.reuters.com. Copyright © 2011 by Reuters. All rights reserved. Reproduced by permission.

"They demanded we allow six of their fighters to board each of our hijacked ships. We have not left our houses since Wednesday. Worse, we are constantly receiving threatening text messages," he said, adding negotiations had begun again.

Islamists clamped down hard on piracy when they briefly ran much of Somalia in 2006, but with ransoms rising they now want a share of its earnings.

Owners of hijacked vessels usually air-drop cash onto the boats and then the pirates disembark.

Despite a flotilla of international warships patrolling the Indian Ocean and Gulf of Aden, pirates continue to rake in tens of millions of dollars in ransoms each year.

Al Shabaab set up an office in Haradheere after last week's deal.

"Negotiations are going on and again I reckon the pirates have no other option but to accept al Shabaab's order," said local elder Ahmed Wardheere, who was involved in negotiations over splitting the ransom.

Magic Powers

Pirates typically target merchant vessels, with oil tankers considered the prize catch, and yachts to get a ransom for their release. But foreign navies have become bolder in launching rescue missions.

As the number of Somali pirates killed by foreign troops on the high seas rises, so too does their hostility towards hijacked crew.

Pirates shot dead four U.S. hostages on a yacht, earlier this month [Februrary 2011], the deadliest incident involving Americans kidnapped for ransom in the increasingly dangerous waters off the Horn of Africa nation. U.S.-forces killed a number of pirates.

One pirate said his colleagues were turning to black magic to counter the mounting perils.

"Some of my colleagues have two sorcerers in Haradheere and Galkayo. These two are expert in explaining the outcome of future hijackings or pending navy attacks by using 'Faal'", a pirate called Hussein said, referring to a local magic where the future is told through markings drawn in the soil.

A sorcerer can earn thousands of dollars and be showered with luxury 4x4 vehicles for accurate predictions that yield a booty for the pirates.

> *Pirates in Haradheere agreed . . . to hand al Shabaab insurgents a 20 percent cut of ransoms.*

The black magic has upset local residents amid rumours the sorcerers are instructing the pirates to sacrifice young children and older women after their comrades died in the shootout with U.S. troops.

"I ran away from the pirates after they killed three men in Hobyo. I heard the next step was to assassinate women who had been through menopause like me," 60-year-old Fatuma Rashid told Reuters by phone from Galkayo.

"And when I arrived in Galkayo, I met mothers worried about their babies. They say they were being hunted by pirates who now believe human killings may be more powerful than slaughtering wild animals."

Pirate Hussein said the sorcerers only request the sacrifice of a rabbit or crocodile to avert death on the ocean.

The Maritime Dimension of International Security: Terrorism, Piracy, and Challenges for the United States: Summary

Peter Chalk

Peter Chalk is a senior political scientist at RAND Corporation, a global research organization based in Santa Monica, California.

Scope and Dimensions

A total of 2,463 actual or attempted acts of piracy were registered around the world between 2000 and the end of 2006. This represents an annual average incident rate of 352, a substantial increase over the mean of 209 recorded for the period of 1994–1999.

The concentration of pirate attacks continues to be greatest in Southeast Asia, especially in the waters around the Indonesian archipelago (including stretches of the Malacca Straits that fall under the territorial jurisdiction of the Jakarta government), which accounted for roughly 25 percent of all global incidents during 2006.

Factors Accounting for the Emergence of Piracy in the Contemporary Era

Seven main factors have contributed to the general emergence of piracy in the contemporary era. First and most fundamentally, there has been a massive increase in commercial mari-

Peter Chalk, "Summary," *The Maritime Dimension of International Security: Terrorism, Piracy, and Challenges for the United States*, RAND, June 5, 2008, pp. xi–xv. www.RAND .org. Copyright © 2008 by RAND Corporation. All rights reserved. Reproduced by permission.

time traffic. Combined with the large number of ports around the world, this growth has provided pirates with an almost limitless range of tempting, high-payoff targets.

Second is the higher incidence of seaborne commercial traffic that passes through narrow and congested maritime chokepoints. These bottlenecks require ships to significantly reduce speed to ensure safe passage, which dramatically heightens their exposure to midsea interception and attack.

Third, and specifically relevant to Southeast Asia, has been the lingering effects of the Asian financial crisis. Not only did this event exert a stronger "pull factor" on piracy—with more people (including members of the security forces) drawn to maritime and other crime—it also deprived many littoral states of the necessary revenue to fund effective monitoring regimes over their coastlines.

Fourth, the general difficulties associated with maritime surveillance have been significantly heightened as a result of the events of September 11, 2001, and the concomitant pressure that has been exerted on many governments to invest in expensive, land-based homeland security initiatives.

Fifth, lax coastal and port-side security have played an important role in enabling low-level piratical activity, especially harbor thefts of goods from ships at anchor.

Sixth, corruption and emergent voids of judicial prerogative have encouraged official complicity in high-level pirate rings, which has impacted directly on the "phantom ship" phenomenon.[1]

Seventh, the global proliferation of small arms has provided pirates (as well as terrorists and other criminal elements) with an enhanced means to operate on a more destructive and sophisticated level.

---

1. The *phantom ship* phenomenon involves the outright hijacking of oceangoing vessels and their re-registration under flags of convenience for the purposes of illicit trade.

The Dangers of Piracy

The dangers associated with contemporary piracy are complex and multifaceted. At the most basic level, attacks constitute a direct threat to the lives and welfare of the citizens of a variety of flag states. Piracy also has a direct economic impact in terms of fraud, stolen cargos, and delayed trips, and could potentially undermine a maritime state's trading ability.

Politically, piracy can play a pivotal role in undermining and weakening regime legitimacy by encouraging corruption among elected government officials. Finally, attacks have the potential to trigger a major environmental disaster, particularly if they take place in crowded sea-lanes traversed by heavily laden oil tankers.

Terrorism

Over the past six years, there has been a modest yet highly discernible spike in high-profile terrorist attacks and plots at sea. These various incidents have galvanized fears in the West that terrorists, especially militants connected with the international jihadist network, are moving to decisively extend operational mandates beyond purely territorially bounded theaters.

Five main factors explain the presumed shift in extremist focus to water-based environments. First, many of the vulnerabilities that have encouraged a higher rate of pirate attacks also apply to terrorism.

Second, the growth of commercial enterprises specializing in maritime sports and equipment has arguably provided terrorists with a readily accessible conduit through which to gain the necessary training and resources for operating at sea.

Third, maritime attacks offer terrorists an alternate means of causing mass economic destabilization. Disrupting the mechanics of the contemporary "just enough, just in time" cargo freight trading system could potentially trigger vast and cascading fiscal effects, especially if the operations of a major commercial port were curtailed.

Fourth, sea-based terrorism constitutes a further means of inflicting mass coercive punishment on enemy audiences. Cruise ships and passenger ferries are especially relevant in this regard because they cater to large numbers of people who are confined in a single physical space.

Complicating the maritime threat picture is growing speculation that a tactical nexus could emerge between piracy and terrorism.

Finally, the expansive global container-shipping complex offers terrorists a viable logistical conduit for facilitating the covert movement of weapons and personnel in two critical respects. First, because much of the maritime trading system is designed to be as accessible and flexible as possible (to keep costs low and turnover high), there is no strong incentive to enact a stringent (and disruptive) regime of security measures. Second, the highly complex nature of the containerized supply chain, combined with the ineffectiveness of point-of-origin inspections, creates a plethora of openings for terrorist infiltration by providing extremists with numerous opportunities to "stuff" or otherwise tamper with boxed crates.

A Terrorism-Piracy Nexus?

Complicating the maritime threat picture is growing speculation that a tactical nexus could emerge between piracy and terrorism. One of the main concerns is that extremist groups will seek to overcome existing operational constraints in sea-based capabilities by working in conjunction with or subcontracting out missions to maritime crime gangs and syndicates.

The presumed convergence between maritime terrorism and piracy remains highly questionable, however. To date, there has been no credible evidence to support speculation about such a nexus emerging. Just as importantly, the objectives of the two actors remain entirely distinct.

That said, the possibility of a possible conflation between piracy and terrorism has informed the perceptions of governments, international organizations, and major shipping interests around the world. There have been persistent reports of political extremists boarding vessels in Southeast Asia in an apparent effort to learn how to pilot them for a rerun of 9/11 at sea. Indeed, such a specter was a principal factor in driving the Lloyd's Joint War Council to briefly designate the Malacca Straits as an area of enhanced risk in 2005.

The presumed convergence between maritime terrorism and piracy remains highly questionable.

Relevance to the United States

The United States has been at the forefront of several moves to upgrade global maritime security over the last five years, including

- the Container Security Initiative

- the International Ship and Port Facility Security (ISPS) Code

- the Proliferation Security Initiative (PSI)

- the Customs-Trade Partnership Against Terrorism.

In addition to these measures, the United States has been instrumental in instituting regional maritime security initiatives and capacity building in areas recognized as vital to U.S. counterterrorism strategy.

On the positive side, these initiatives have helped to lend a degree of transparency to what has hitherto been a highly opaque theater. On the negative side, these programs suffer from three critical shortfalls as presently configured:

- They are limited in scope.

- They are largely directed at strengthening the security "wall" around commercial seaborne traffic, paying scant attention to contingencies that do not involve containerized cargo.

- With particular reference to the ISPS Code, there is still no definitive means of effectively auditing how well extant measures are being implemented by participating states or, indeed, to gauge their overall utility in terms of dock-side security.

Policy Recommendations

At the policy level, there are at least four major contributions that the United States could make to better safeguard the global oceanic environment, including the following: (1) helping to further expand the nascent regime of post-9/11 maritime security; (2) informing the parameters of bilateral and multilateral maritime security collaboration by conducting regular and rigorous threat assessments; (3) assisting with redefining mandates of existing multilateral security and defense arrangements to allow them to play a more effective and inclusive role in countering maritime (and other transnational) threats; and (4) encouraging the commercial maritime industry to make greater use of enabling communication and defensive technologies and accept a greater degree of transparency in its corporate structures.

In more specific terms, U.S. funds and support could be usefully directed at (1) boosting the coastal monitoring and interdiction capabilities of states in areas of strategic maritime importance; (2) actively supporting the International Maritime Bureau's piracy reporting center in Malaysia; (3) augmenting port security management; and (4) sponsoring research into cost-effective initiatives for better securing ships and oceanic freight.

Somali Pirates Do Not Appear to Be Connected to the Somali Islamist Movement

Karine Hamilton

Karine Hamilton is a research fellow at Australia's Edith Cowan University, where she coordinates various research projects in the fields of family justice, community wellbeing, crime prevention, and policing.

Since 2008, piracy off the coast of Somalia has captured world headlines. The International Maritime Bureau (IMB) reported 406 pirate attacks around the world in 2009, of which over half were conducted by Somalis. In 2010, the number of Somali pirate attacks appears to have decreased slightly due to the impact of international navy patrols off Somalia's coastline and also due to the use of better defences by vessels travelling through affected waters. Nonetheless, Somali pirates are adjusting to naval patrols by launching attacks in higher seas, and the waters around Somalia are still the most pirate-risky in the world: 100 pirate attacks and 27 hijackings were reported around Somalia during the first 6 months of 2010.

Most analysts and journalists have interpreted Somali piracy as an economic venture, however a significant number have speculated that it is linked to terrorism. For example, two analysts recently wrote that "piracy on the high seas is currently becoming key tactics of terrorist groups—many of today's pirates are also terrorists with ideological bents and a broad political agenda". The sorts of maritime terrorist acts that have been hypothesised include the use of ships as floating bombs to ram other vessels or carry explosives; attacks

Karine Hamilton, "The Piracy and Terrorism Nexus: Real or Imagined?," *Journal of the Australia Institute of Professional Intelligence Officers*, 2011. Copyright © 2011 by *Journal of the Australia Institute of Professional Intelligence Officers*. All rights reserved. Reproduced by permission.

against ferry or cruise ships to kill large numbers of civilians; jamming thin water passages to obstruct trade; and, causing deliberate environmental catastrophes such as oil spills.

Defining Piracy and Terrorism

Both 'piracy' and 'terrorism' are terms that have been subject to ongoing debate about their definition and legal meanings. The 1958 Convention on the High Seas defines *piracy* as any of the following acts:

(1) Any illegal acts of violence, detention or any act of depredation, committed for private ends by the crew or the passengers of a private ship or a private aircraft, and directed:

(a) On the high seas, against another ship or aircraft, or against persons or property on board such ship or aircraft;

(b) Against a ship, aircraft, persons or property in a place outside the jurisdiction of any State.

Even in the event that a connection between piracy and [Somalian Islamist terrorist group] Shabaab was confirmed, it would not automatically relate to the global war on terror.

On the other hand *maritime terrorism* refers to "any illegal act directed against ships, their passengers, cargo or crew, or against sea ports with the intent of directly or indirectly influencing a government or group of individuals". These two definitions highlight that the key distinction between piracy and maritime terrorism relates to motivation. Pirates are motivated by "private ends", generally financial gain, whilst maritime terrorists are politically motivated and they aim to influence government policy through the use or threat of violence. . . .

A Loose Connection, If Any

Even though certain elements within Shabaab [Somalian Islamist group associated with terrorism] are increasingly aligning their objectives with [Islamic terrorist network] Al Qaeda, the affiliation between the two groups is loose. On the whole, the rise of Shabaab and its use of violence internally and abroad largely relates to Somalia's domestic and regional conflicts rather than to the conflict between America and Al Qaeda. Hence even in the event that a connection between piracy and Shabaab was confirmed, it would not automatically relate to the global war on terror.

Regardless, a connection between pirates and terrorism has never been clearly established. Geographically, pirates and Islamists are largely based separately from each other. The Shabaab operates in south-central Somalia and the pirates are mostly based further along the coast, especially around Puntland in northern Somalia. The occasions that pirates and Islamists have had contact have shown that any relationship between them is one of dispute and confrontation. The period during which the Islamic Courts Union [ICU] came to power in Mogadishu during 2006 effectively ended piracy in the region. The ICU publicly outlawed piracy and declared it as *Haraam* or anti-Islamic: threatening death or amputation for any Somali caught in the act of piracy. The ICU initiated an offensive against ports used by pirates which led to pirates being injured, expelled or left in hiding. Pirate attacks from the area had averaged around 40 a year prior to the ICU and none were recorded whilst the ICU was in power. The Ethiopian intervention which terminated ICU enabled pirate groups to regroup.

There are other instances of open dispute between Islamists and pirates in Somalia. In 2008, pirates captured the *Sirius Star*, a super-tanker from Saudi Arab that was carrying 100 million dollars worth of crude oil. The Islamic Courts Union condemned the capture as a "major crime". More vehemently a Shabaab leader informed journalists that "Saudi is a Muslim country, and it is a very big crime to hold Muslim property ... I warned again and again, those who hold the ship must free it unconditionally or armed conflict should be the solution. If they don't free the ship, we will rescue it by force". One of the pirates involved clarified with a journalist that: "Every Somali has great respect for the holy kingdom of Saudi Arabia. We have nothing against them but unfortunately what happened was just business for us and I hope the Saudis will understand". The Shabaab sent armoured vehicles loaded with armed fighters to the pirate's base, the port town Harardhere, and the pirates fled to avoid direct confrontation. The incident highlights the economic motivations behind piracy and the hostility between pirates and Islamists in Somalia.

More recently, in April of this year (2010), the chief pirate base Harardhere (located mid-way along the Somali coast) was taken over by the Islamic group Hizbul Islam, which is Shabaab's main rival. Shabaab itself had tried to take the port town but locals instead invited Shabaab's rival Hizbul Islam who proceeded to drive pirates out of the town. A Hizbul Islam member was quoted: "Piracy has become too much. It's an anti-Islamic business, and we won't accept it ... We want to bring law and order to that country of Somalia, and we want to show the good name of Somalis". Both Shabaab and Hizbul Islam were angered by recent pirate attacks on Indian ships which had disrupted the flow of further Indian cargoes into Somalia; ships that had been an important source of revenue by way of port tariffs in Islamic controlled ports. Essentially, Islamic groups want to rid coastal towns of pirates in order to secure an important revenue stream in the form of ship tariffs. In the nearby coastal town which the pirates fled to, Hobyo, pirates were recently enlisted by local officials to act as an armed defence against Shabaab and Hizbul Islam. Pirate leaders in Hobyo claim to have deliberately amassed a significant on-land arsenal of militiamen and weapons in order to ward off Shabaab and Hizbul Islam.

A Consensus Opinion

While conducting research in Kenya where over 100 Somalis accused of piracy are currently imprisoned and undergoing prosecution, I found general consensus that Somali piracy was unrelated to Islamic politics and was instead strictly an economic crime. The main aim of the research was to interview imprisoned Somalis in order to understand their motivations for piracy, however all but one of them refused to admit to engaging in piracy and instead claimed to be either fishermen or people smugglers. Almost all of the prisoners interviewed came from Bosaso, which is Somalia's chief port city located in Puntland and is known for its fishing and illegal immigrant industries. A small number of the pirates came from in or around Mogadishu. Aside from these imprisoned Somalis accused of being pirates, we spoke to other key stakeholders such as European Union [EU] personnel and Kenyan police and judicial officials involved in prosecuting pirate cases.

Islamic groups want to rid coastal towns [in Somalia] of pirates in order to secure an important revenue stream in the form of ship tariffs.

In general, talking to Kenyans about the purpose of my research, it was obviously common knowledge that the Somali community was financially benefitting from the pirate industry. Kenyans, and Somalis, were quick to point to flashy new residential homes known to be owned and inhabited by Somalis and explained that it was usual for Somalis to buy whole apartment buildings at exorbitant prices and then demolish and rebuild from scratch. The money financing these redevelopments was understood to partly come from piracy, which was only ever spoken about in terms of its obvious financial profits for Somalis.

People more directly involved with the prosecution of pirate cases in Kenya concurred. The police officer in charge of investigating pirate cases in Kenya explained that "these people are looking for money". A British naval officer stationed in Kenya stated that "I would suspect that they [Somali pirates] see it as business". This Naval Officer and an EU-appointed lawyer who liaised with Kenyan judicial officials had both de-briefed hostages after their release from Somali pirate captors and none had ever indicated that their Somali captors are motivated by anything other than economic consideration. According to the EU lawyer,

> apparently some of the pirate guards are quite vocal about talking with the hostages and its frankly to get them and their families out of Somalia and to another country, . . . I want to make this much and then I will get out.

In his role, he never came across a hostage who heard their Somali captors make reference to any ideological or religious motivations for their actions; rather they confided to the hostages that they wanted to improve their lives. The one Somali prisoner in Kenya who admitted to being a pirate during interviewing corroborated this picture by stating that his chief concern was to get a proper education whilst he was in jail, principally he was keen to learn English as the international language. He wanted to leave prison in a better position to make something of his life and he was motivated by wanting a better life.

The navy officer who likewise had spoken to hostages post-release concurred that Somali pirates were quite talkative about their motivations to their hostages and they never mentioned Islam or wider conflicts between East and West. Instead, Somali captors told their hostages that "they wanted to get x thousand, x one thousand dollars, uh false documents cost this much, however there are so many members of my family". In short, Somalis in communication with their hostages made it clear that they were seeking money in order to better their lives. In terms of pirate attitudes towards their hostages, there was mistreatment but not of a systematic directed kind, more along the lines of not allowing them to shower and keeping them in cramped living spaces. Injuries and fatalities amongst hostages have been accidental. Whilst pirates treat their hostages badly as a way of putting pressure on ransom payments, they are quite strict about not harming the hostages and compromising ransom payments. For these reasons, the individuals involved in prosecuting Somalis accused of piracy all took the view that pirates were motivated by financial gain and that the phenomenon of piracy from Somalia was strictly an economic crime.

Somali piracy is unrelated to terrorism and stems from financial ambitions.

A Lack of Cooperation

Current knowledge about the nature of terrorism and piracy in Somalia all point toward the conclusion that the two phenomena are distinct from each other both in terms of geography and practice. Moreover the history of Shabaab, the Islamic group most strongly associated with terrorism, shows that it emerged and developed quite separately from piracy in Somalia. Shabaab's recent alliance with Al Qaeda remains disputed within the group itself which means that establishing a clear connection between Somali pirates and Shabaab does not necessarily entail an obvious link between piracy and the War on Terror. So far, Shabaab's agendas have clearly curtailed piracy whenever it has come into a position of power within a pirate-active location. Overall, the two groups appear more in competition with each other over access to ports and money than they appear in any form of cooperation. The research that I conducted in Kenya, whilst obviously restricted by the informal nature of my sources of information, likewise indicated that Somali piracy is unrelated to terrorism and stems from financial ambitions.

The Somali Islamist Group al-Shabaab Actually Deters Somali Piracy

Somalia Report

Somalia Report is a news service that works with Somali journalists and international experts to provide insight and nonpartisan news coverage of the region.

A FRICOM [US African Command, a Department of Defense agency focused on Africa] commander Gen. Carter F. Ham recently touted the old line that there are links between militant Islamist group al-Shabaab and piracy, but there is little evidence to support such assertions and the actions of the group seem to point in the opposite direction.

Ham can be excused, since the General has been in the AFRICOM saddle less than a month, but US policy heads commonly drop in a casual mention about the link between piracy and terrorism. [US diplomat] Johnnie Carson mentioned that piracy was becoming a transnational problem when he discovered that Yemenis were among the pirates who killed the four American yachtsmen on the *SV Quest.* He seems to have forgotten the proximity and common linkages between mariners of both neighboring nations.

Despite quips that seem to convey confirmation of "the third rail", Ham has his sights on the right target.

"There has to be a whole-government approach," he said, "to deal with their finances and to deal with their activities on shore."

Carson also has a firm grip on the realities of the Somali situation by pulling back from the TFG [Somalia's transitional

"OP-ED: Al-Shabaab, Pirates and the West," *Somalia Report*, April 9, 2011. Somalia Report.com. Copyright © 2011 by *Somalia Report*. All rights reserved. Reproduced by permission.

federal government] and engaging more-successful, less-time-consuming political partners in the troubled country. But these off-hand comments seem to be attempts to tie ideological, political or religious terrorism to a crime that is driven purely by profit.

Terrorist Groups Not Linked to Piracy

The most "conclusive" evidence of an al-Shabaab [link to pirates] was presented in December of 2009, when Canadian Intelligence was convinced the group was arming and training pirates in exchange for a slice of the pie.

The Top Secret report by Integrated Threat Assessment Centre maintained that there was an "Islamist extremism-piracy nexus" with al-Shabaab providing "weapons, combat training and local protection" to the Mudug pirates of southern Somalia. In exchange, al-Shabaab was to receive a percentage of the ransoms.

Al-Shabaab is neither a maritime-based group nor do its leaders know anything about the dark secrets of negotiating ransoms with insurance companies.

The concept is questionable considering that the locations, skillset and purpose of piracy requires very specific maritime hostile-boarding skills, coastal access and sailing history (al-Shabaab recruits primary from inland camps and southern areas) and also patient ransom negotiation skills with insurance companies or ship owners. Sure, some pirate new hires may have learned how to shoot a gun in al-Shabaab camps, but they can get the same training from the TFG, Puntland [a region in Somalia] Marines, foreign countries and other training programs. The ideology does not transfer, even if the skills do.

Al-Shabaab is neither a maritime-based group nor do its leaders know anything about the dark secrets of negotiating ransoms with insurance companies. This skill was nurtured in Bosasso during a maritime security training program that fell apart in 2000. If al-Shabaab had these skills, and evidence could be presented, it would make the venerable British maritime insurance providers direct supporters of terrorists and subject to numerous financial, travel and criminal sanctions.

The rumor of links between pirates and terrorists first surfaced in 2008, when al-Shabaab demanded weapons from the hijacked *MV Faina* and were rebuffed, then again in 2009 upon the release of a *Jane's Defense Weekly* report. It also came up in 2010 when al-Shabaab tried to take over [the Somalian pirate-base town of] Haradhere, but were repelled. In September 2010, Sheikh Mahad Omar Abdikarim, head of Bay and Bakool regions, was reported to have made a call for a "sea jihad" and called upon fighters to attack American ships.

"We have to retaliate against them by sea or by land," an anonymous source quoted him as saying.

Residents of Kismayo and Barawe insist they saw armed al-Shabaab fighters heading out to sea. Six months later, the lack of any action or proof makes the story seem as foolish as it originally sounded.

Al-Shabaab's Slice of the Pie

But back to the genesis of this rumor. It comes from no other than Ambassadorial level. Specifically, the very experienced Ambassador David Shinn, now an adjunct professor at the Elliot School of International Affairs at Washington University. It appears that Ambassador Shinn ignored his many years in Somalia and adopted this report in a number of Somalia-related public presentations.

He insisted in his speeches that al-Shabaab requires pirates to pay a protection fee of 5 to 10 per cent of any ransom money collected. Additionally, he maintains that if al-Shabaab helps to train the pirates, they receive 20 per cent. He goes on to say that al-Shabaab's share can be as high as 50 per cent if they financed the operation.

These "facts" actually comes from a *Jane's Defense Weekly* report, and in reality Ambassador Shinn does not believe there is a direct link between the two groups. His exact quote is: "Let me begin with two caveats. First, all of my information comes from open sources; those of you with access to classified information on this subject may be disappointed with some of the lacunae [gaps] in my presentation. The best open-source reporting I have seen on this topic comes from *Jane's Intelligence Review*."

In the same speech, the ambassador claims a reverse connection: that the pirates actually provide weapons to al-Shabaab using their Yemeni connections: "There is increasing evidence that the pirates are assisting al-Shabaab with arms smuggling from Yemen and two central Asian countries."

In January of this year [2011] Vice Adm. Mark Fox, commander of the Navy's Bahrain-based Central Command fleet, stated that "al-Shabaab is responsible for a lot of training activity and camps and that sort of thing in Somalia."

The truth is that al-Shabaab has been the only effective land-based deterrent to piracy.

He neatly broke piracy into eight "action groups", each with a mother ship and pirates.

"There cannot be segregation between terrorist activity, in my mind, and counter-piracy. We can't be passive and hopeful it doesn't happen. I'm not advocating we suddenly just come out with guns blazing and just change everything," said Fox. "But I would advocate that we used the same techniques that have been successful in our counter-terror that we have not heretofore used in our counter-piracy."

Thankfully he does point out that piracy is currently being treated as a law-enforcement activity.

It would appear that the pirates and al-Shabaab are everywhere.

Islamists as Piracy Deterrent

The reality is that local militias like Ali Osman Atto provide land security, and the few weapons that are needed by pirates (they are usually rusted and old) are shipped and purchased through the al-Shabaab-controlled port in Kismayo.

The real relationship is best defined by the April 8, 2011 attack on Haradhere by al-Shabaab, which drove the pirates north to Hobyo. Those pirates that didn't flee were arrested by the Islamic group. Al-Shabaab views the pirates as corrosive to their main source of income, which is the port taxes and shipment of goods in Kismayo. The pirates view al-Shabaab as the third rail that will bring down the wrath of America's well-oiled terrorist killing machine.

The truth is that al-Shabaab has been the only effective land-based deterrent to piracy and the one group that has actively driven them out of pirate 'dens' like Haradhere. Not only have they forced the pirates to move their ships far north of Kismayo and Mogadishu, but they have arrested at least 50 pirates in Haradhere—a direct contrast to more apocryphal media stories about al-Shabaab demanding that they have at least two fighters on every pirate ship to ensure fair payment.

To date we have found no proof of piracy linked with al-Qaeda, al-Shabaab or terrorism.

Does al-Shabaab get money from pirates? Yes and no. Al-Shabaab is a divided, diverse group that holds sway in the vacuum of any functioning Somalia government. There can be no doubt that at some point pirate money crosses al-Shabaab hands. But does al-Shabaab dictate, control or fund piracy? Somalia Report has seen no evidence of this, and believes that the two groups are mutually toxic to each other's existence.

The insurgents exist to rid Somalia of outsiders, criminals and western influence. Pirates rely on outsiders, criminals and western influence.

We continue to investigate, probe and keep an open mind, but to date we have found no proof of piracy linked with al-Qaeda, al-Shabaab or terrorism. Could the act of piracy be re-defined as a terrorist act? Possibly, since the mass kidnapping of innocent multinationals and now the murder of four Americans is terror, but no political, ideological or religious demands have ever been made by pirates. They want money. Pure and simple.

Then there is the very real threat that any hard linkage of piracy to terrorism could unleash the full impact of the US anti-terrorism forces in the region. The US has not been shy about shelling, bombing, shooting and hunting down anyone linked to al-Qaeda. For now, the pundits' favorite fantasy of supertankers being steered by khat-addled [drug-crazed] sui-cidal jihadis is still in the realm of Hollywood scriptwriters.

Piracy can only survive as an embarrassingly amoral rela-tionship between ransom payers and ship takers. Each party dutifully maintains a false sense of purpose to condone their acts. The pirates insist they are protecting the seas and the in-surance companies insist they are ensuring the safe delivery of crew, ship and cargo. But they both make profits by dancing with the devil. Al-Shabaab has not been invited onto the dance floor.

CHAPTER 3

Should Ransoms Be Paid to Pirates?

Chapter Preface

The majority of pirate attacks in recent years have not involved the torture or killing of hostages or the confiscating of cargo but rather the capture and holding of hostages, cargo, and ships until a ransom is paid to obtain their release. In February 2011, however, four Americans were shot to death by pirates after their private yacht, the *Quest*, was hijacked off the coast of Somalia. The dead Americans included the yacht's owners, Californians Jean and Scott Adam, and two passengers from Seattle, Wash., Bob Riggle and Phyllis Macay. The four had been part of an international yacht race but they had left the race early to deliver Bibles to various locations around the world. Many commentators say this incident suggests that Somalia pirates are becoming more violent than in the past, and more likely to kill hostages.

According to reports, the *Quest* hijacking began with Somali pirates cruising the ocean in a hijacked Yemeni ship, with Yemeni hostages on board, looking for another ship to attack. Once they found the *Quest*, eighteen Somali pirates, armed with AK-47s and other weapons, and one Yemeni man who had joined them boarded the *Quest* and took the four Americans hostage, releasing the Yemeni vessel and hostages. While the pirates were sailing the *Quest* and the hostages back to Somalia to begin ransom negotiations, however, they were intercepted by a US warship, a destroyer named the USS *Sterett*. The warship followed the yacht for three days while US Special Forces planned a rescue.

Negotiations were also initiated with the pirates. At one point, one of the pirates, Mohamud Salad Ali, boarded the US Navy ship to discuss matters and was offered a deal—the pirates would be allowed to return to Somalia on the *Quest* if they let the Americans go. Ali refused the deal, and was arrested. As these negotiations were being concluded, however, and before Special Forces could attempt a rescue, a rocket-propelled grenade was shot at the warship about the same time as a gunfight broke out among the pirates on the *Quest*. Reportedly, some of the pirates decided to massacre the Americans after the *Sterett* sent a radio message to the *Quest* that it would prevent the yacht from being moved to Somalia. The end result was that four of the pirates and the four Americans, who were being held in the *Quest*'s wheelhouse, were shot and killed. Special Forces soldiers immediately boarded the yacht and tried to save the lives of the American sailors, but they were mortally wounded and later died of their wounds.

The pirates who were not killed in the gunfight, thirteen Somalis and one Yemeni, were taken into custody by US soldiers and brought to the United States for prosecution. They were indicted by a grand jury and charged with piracy, kidnapping, and firearms crimes. On May 23, 2011, three of the Somali defendants—including the pirate negotiator, the pirate who fired the rocket-propelled grenade, and another pirate leader—appeared in a Virginia court to plead guilty to piracy and hostage-taking, but said in their plea agreements that they did not participate in any direct way in the killings. Two other defendants pled guilty two days later. The men pled guilty in order to avoid the death penalty, but all five will face a mandatory life sentence for their crimes. Their sentencings were scheduled for dates in August, September, and October 2011. The remaining defendants were scheduled to appear in court at a later date.

Some commentators have reported that Somali pirates have vowed to kill hostages in the future if attempts are made to rescue the hostages or attack their ships. If this becomes the trend, it will signal a dangerous escalation of violence and seriousness associated with Somalia piracy. This may be happening, experts say, because piracy has become so lucrative that criminal gangs are now entering the fray. Although the average ransom paid to pirates just a few years ago was in the hundreds of thousands of dollars, the average ransom today stands at about $5 million. And recently one ransom of close to $10 million was paid to pirates. The new criminal breed of pirates, many people fear, are likely to be much more organized and violent than the Somali fishermen who used to make up the piracy gangs. Authors in this chapter debate the critical question of whether ransoms should be paid to pirates.

Pirates Treat Hostages Well If Ransoms Are Paid

Center for Strategic and International Studies

The Center for Strategic and International Studies is a public policy research institution that provides analysis and policy advice to decisionmakers in governments, international organizations, the private sector, and others.

On Sunday, April 12, [2009,] U.S. Navy snipers fatally shot three pirates holding an American cargo-ship captain hostage, marking a change in U.S.-Somali pirate relations. The ship's captain, Richard Phillips, safely returned to the USS *Bainbridge*, and the operation was deemed a success. President [Barack] Obama used the occasion to voice his intention to "remain resolved to halt the rise of piracy in this region" by holding pirates "accountable for their crimes".

President Obama's new policy orientation is shortsighted. While rescuing an American citizen and reuniting him with his family is certainly joyous in and of itself, the ramifications from this episode and attached declarations will likely aggravate an already difficult situation.

So Long Humane Treatment

The decision to kill the pirates redefines the stakes and endangers present and future hostages. Unlike such ideologically motivated enemies as al Qaeda, Somali pirates engaged in illicit activities for purely economic purposes. As long as they received ransom, the pirates actually treated their hostages quite well, "sometimes roasting goat meat for them and even passing phones round so they can call loved ones. The worst

Center for Strategic and International Studies, "Tread Carefully," CSIS.org, May 16, 2011. Copyright © 2011 by Center for Strategic and International Studies (CSIS). All rights reserved. Reproduced by permission.

violence reported has been the occasional beating and no hostages are known to have been killed by pirates".

Americans can now likely kiss such humane treatment goodbye. According to Andrew Mwangura, coordinator of Mombasa-based East African Seafarers Assistance Program, "This is a big wake-up [call] to the pirates. It raises the stakes. Now they may be more violent, like the pirates of old". Indeed, on Monday, April 13th, Abdullahi Ahmed, a member of a pirate group based in Haradhere, told a Somalia journalist, "We have decided to kill U.S. and French sailors if they happen to be among our future hostages." Another pirate, Ali Nur, stated, "From now on, after the killings by the U.S. and France, we will add some harsher steps in our dealings with hostages, particularly American and French hostages".

Thus, the new status quo taking shape appears to be Somali pirates intending to harm specifically American hostages and President Obama intending to confront and hold them accountable for their actions. Unfortunately for President Obama, this is a wholly untenable position.

Somali pirates engaged in illicit activities for purely economic purposes. As long as they received ransom, the pirates actually treated their hostages quite well.

Piracy Rooted in Poverty

Given the situation on the ground in Somalia, piracy appears for many to be one of few viable options for economic improvement. For some, piracy stems from necessity not choice. Take for example Mohammad, a father of six children: "Tired of lacking prospects, living in a crumbling house and walking in fear of the ever-present militias in Galkayo ... [he] plan[s] to join the pirates in Kobyo, who had sent him money for his travel, 'My children are dying of hunger,' he says. 'I no longer have a choice.' He dreams of marrying two new young, beautiful wives, and 'everyone knows that piracy is the only activity around here that pays well." President Obama must understand that Somali piracy is not some choice that a few bad apples are making—it is a rational act stemming from extreme desperation and a complete lack of any other viable option to improve one's own life. Piracy is a function of a greater systemic problem—focusing on it is simply trying to combat a symptom while ignoring the disease. As such, piracy will last as long as Somalia remains a festering failed state. . . .

Piracy in Somalia will not stop until there is real progress on land. Unless President Obama wants to introduce a large-scale operation (through aid and development) to address the most anarchic place in the world, his threats will remain misplaced, and American sailors' lives will stay endangered.

Paying Ransoms Is the Only Available Response to Piracy for Ship Owners

Charles Marts

Charles Marts is a student in the class of 2012 at Tulane University Law School in New Orleans. His interests lie in maritime law and energy law.

"Currently the only avenue available to the ship owner [for the release of pirated boats or hostages] is the payment of ransom," argues Cyrus Mody, Manager of the International Maritime Bureau (IMB), a body established in 1981 to act as a focal point in the fight against maritime crime and malpractice. Prohibiting ransoms is ill-considered [as] it eliminates a proven tool for hostage resolution, putting crews and vessels at risk. Paying ransoms promotes the continued humane treatment of merchant seafarers that are captured, is cost effective, and limits risk of environmental disasters.

Yet despite these benefits of paying the ransom, a spate of recent policy development by the United States, the European Union, and the United Nations appears to limit this proven ability to secure the release of a captured vessel quickly and peacefully.

Pirates who have successfully hijacked a ship are able to threaten its destruction or violence to the crew. This leverage leaves government and military authorities with very few opportunities for rescue without incurring significant risks. Naval forces generally abstain from recapturing vessels despite their overwhelming firepower except on limited occasions because of the risk of endangering the lives of the crew aboard.

Charles Marts, "Chapter One: Pro-Ransom—Maritime Industry Prospective," *Piracy Ransoms—Conflicting Perspectives*, One Earth Future, August 13, 2010, pp. 7–17. www.OneEarthFuture.org. Copyright © 2010 by One Earth Future. All rights reserved. Reproduced by permission.

Efforts at diplomacy are plagued by the lack of an authority in Somalia willing or capable of dealing with the pirates. Justice David Steel of the Queen's Bench [in the United Kingdom] has recognized that "[in Somalia] any attempt to intervene by diplomatic means is fraught with difficulty." As both alternate avenues for resolution are so hindered, the justice noted that: "In short the only realistic and effective manner of obtaining the release of a vessel is the negotiation and payment of a ransom."

Given the existing constraints on the ability of public actors to rectify the general and specific incidents of piracy, it makes little sense to remove the only avenue open to the ship owner. In a specific hijacking incident a ship owner stands to lose the ship [and] the crew, and to suffer financial burdens. Anti-ransom policies only add legal burdens to these complications. As the primary users of the high seas, ship owners, cargo owners, and insurers are the largest stakeholders in general incidents of piracy. Keeping the means of release within their control allows them to best manage the risks and rewards of transiting through the designated high-risk zones. . . .

The only realistic and effective manner of obtaining the release of a vessel is the negotiation and payment of a ransom.

Humanitarian Reasons for Paying

Somali piracy is unique because it functions under a model of kidnap and ransom in which hostages are taken and traded for payments. The United Nations [UN] Monitoring Group on Somalia, in its report of August 22, 2005, to the UN Security Council, stated that the aim of the attacks on ships sailing off the coast of Somalia is to secure ransom demands.

Under the current model, ransoms are extracted by leveraging the lives of the hijacked crew. Roger Middleton, an expert on Somali piracy at Chatham House [in the United Kingdom] notes, "The reality in Somalia is that the pirates are not trying to steal the cargo or the ship itself—they're trying to take control of crew so they can ransom them." Somali pirates claim openly that the revenues generated from acts of piracy are used for their own sustenance. After hijacking the Ukrainian freighter *Faina* loaded with a cargo of arms and tanks in September of 2008, Somali pirate spokesman Sugule Ali said that the pirates had no plans to offload the weapons: "We just want the money."

Although the situation is admittedly distasteful, the Somali pirates have consistently upheld their promises, and after capturing vessels have conducted themselves with a modicum of respect for the crew and with professionalism in negotiations. After the release of the French yacht *Le Ponant*, Agence France Presse reported that a pirate *Good Conduct Guide*, outlining appropriate methods for hostage treatment, was found onboard. If there is anything good about the Somali piracy it is that for right now it is a predictable business transaction. The hijackers are more interested in the ransom money than trying to sell the cargo or ship. When ransoms are paid, the pirates release the ship, crew, and cargo.

> *When ransoms are paid, the pirates release the ship, crew, and cargo.*

The highly publicized case of the Chandlers, a British yachting couple captured by Somali pirates on October 23, 2009, and still held today due to their inability to pay a ransom, illustrates the professionalism of the Somali model. Despite threats and the emotional toll, the pirates have provided the Chandlers with modest medical attention and some respite as the situation has progressed.

To date [August 2010], Somali pirates have not made a practice of torturing or killing crews of hijacked vessels. This would seem to be a logically necessary component of the kidnap and ransom model. Because Somali pirates are in the business for money alone, it is in their interest to make sure hostages survive. According to Sugule Ali, spokesman for the pirates who hijacked the *Faina*, "Killing is not in our plans."

To minimize provocation of violent incidents, merchant mariners are now trained and counseled to offer no resistance once pirates are onboard the vessel. Mona Intong, director of Marlow Navigation's government-mandated anti-piracy training program for Filipino mariners stated, "Apparently, the pirates do not wish to harm the crew inasmuch as they will expect to get a better ransom term if no member is dead." However, she did note that the treatment of captured mariners is still far from humane. The pirates do observe decorum despite a degree of emotional and psychological stress on the crews and their families.

No Safe Alternatives

Existing alternative models lack respect for hostage lives

In most other regions of the world the target of pirate attacks is not the crew. Off the west coast of Africa piracy is generally conducted under a different model, *political terror and criminal opportunism*. Nigerian pirates claim affiliation with the Movement for the Emancipation of the Niger Delta (MEND), and proclaim to be motivated by a political desire to regain control of the region's oil reserves from multinational corporations. They employ violence and "terror" tactics.

In the Niger Delta, marauders in armed speedboats attack tankers and work with militants in the delta swamplands. Unlike Somali pirates, who do not convincingly claim to be perpetrating the crime for any objective beyond a better standard of living for themselves, the motivations of MEND and the copycat criminals are obfuscated by political demands. Rather than utilize the somewhat complicated and slow Somali kidnap and ransom model, funding for Nigerian pirates is largely derived from the illegal sale of fuel stolen from aboveground pipelines in the delta region. The attacks are notable for the willingness of the pirates to use violence. This is a model of political terror, which often deteriorates into simple violent robbery.

Though there are some incidents of kidnapping by the Niger Delta pirates, they have generally rejected ransoms and instead sought political concessions. Of 21 pirate-boarding incidents reported in Nigeria during 2009, only one vessel was hijacked. Instead, piratical attacks are focused on stealing ship equipment and crew belongings, such as in the recent attack on the cargo ship *M/V North Spirit* off Cameroon.

In Southeast Asia, the kill and sell cargo model is commonly employed. In the case of the Japanese bulk carrier *Tenyu*, the vessel was stolen only to be recovered months later after having been repainted and re-flagged. The cargo was gone and the crew was presumed dead. These ships are repainted and reflagged and often used as "phantom ships" for illegal trade. Although it may be difficult to sell some cargos due to storage and handling constraints, cargo nevertheless remains an alternate source of income or vehicle for threat of disaster.

In contrast with the rarity of injury and death among victims of Somali pirates, the incidents of Nigerian pirate attacks regularly leave dead and wounded. IMB Director Pottengal Mukundan has recognized that "[t]he attacks in Nigerian waters are frequently much more violent in nature than those off Somalia." Additionally, "[t]he incidence of violent attacks against ships' crews has also recently spilled over into neighboring states." The low threshold for restraint against violence is likely due to the diminished value of the hijacked crews in the eyes of their captors.

The risk of minimizing the value of each crew life is a significant problem. Under an alternate model, the likelihood that each crewmember would be seen as a liability to the pirates instead of an asset for recovery of ransom would be high. Currently, a Philippine government order requires all merchant mariners to attend anti-piracy training. This is a commendable and important measure for defense, but in addition one could imagine requirements for also training merchant seamen in offensive tactics due to escalating violence against mariners if ransoms are prohibited. As director of one of these mandated programs, Mona Intong thinks a refusal to pay ransoms will lead to increased deaths on both sides. She worries that violence against mariners would escalate, and there would be difficulty predicting what training would be required to protect mariners against violence once pirates have boarded.

If the traditional payoff [of ransoms] is eliminated . . . Somali pirates may seek an alternate form of revenue generation that most likely will be less conducive to peaceful resolution.

It is too risky to alter the Somali model without a clear alternative.

If the traditional payoff is eliminated from the existing kidnap and ransom model, Somali pirates may seek an alternate form of revenue generation that most likely will be less conducive to peaceful resolution. These alternatives may have the effect of making the captors less willing to care for hijacked crews. International Chamber of Shipping Marine Director Peter Hinchliffe has estimated that as of April 27, 2010, as many as 300 merchant mariners were being held hostage and their lives would be put at risk with a ban on ransom payments.

Stephen Carmel of the Danish shipping company Maersk believes that Somali pirates are likely to test the resolve of those ship owners unwilling to pay ransoms. By holding multiple hostages, Somali pirates have the potential to publicly and horrifically sacrifice captives one at a time until the resolve of the nation prohibiting payment falters. Despite prohibition, a ship owner may simply decide that paying a ransom for crew release and incurring any prosecutorial liability will be a better option than allowing his employees to be harmed. The ship owner would probably argue that he acted under duress. This is an argument that would likely have merit.

Trying More-Dangerous Models

As rational actors exploiting a "business" model, Somali pirates are employing a strategy with proven success. However, a restriction on their ability to derive ransom payments will most likely prompt them to alter their strategy to maintain their accustomed reward. There are already signs that pirates have been taking a certain portion of hostages to be held in captivity ashore as reciprocity for the arrest of Somali pirate suspects by foreign naval powers, and as leverage for their exchange.

Pirate organizations could turn from the kidnap and ransom model to a capture, kill, and sell cargo model similar to Nigeria or Southeast Asia. The possibility of an illicit trade in hijacked goods exists throughout Somalia no less than it does anywhere else in the world. Buyers may participate willingly, or may be unable to resist low prices and so are unwilling to ask too many questions. [Researcher Roy] Love notes that "[a] high degree of informal economic interconnectedness exists across the entire Horn [of Africa] region, underpinning the ability of market forces to adapt and connect across borders, and of their participants to establish mechanisms of payment and receipt of goods which can function outside the formal sector. . . ." In addition to potential ruthless treatment of captured crews, this would create a secondary source of enforcement challenges in trying to apprehend dealers of black market goods.

Perhaps even more frightening is the concern that if pirates are unable to derive ransoms from ship owners or insurance policies, they may seek payments from other organizations willing to pay to take control of the captives. Though there is little evidence of links between Somali pirates and terrorism, frightening scenarios are not beyond imagination. Roger Middleton of Chatham House emphasizes that incidents of "seaborne terrorism" need to be taken seriously. An organization such as al-Shabaab or al-Qaeda (with whom al-Shabaab claims to be linked) may find it affordable and strategically useful to "purchase" pirate captives for political manipulation or terror. Though as yet there are no known cases of this happening to mariners, Al Qaeda has purchased and subsequently executed at least one captured tourist in Mali when efforts to exchange him for a radical cleric imprisoned in the UK [United Kingdom] failed. Additionally, a report claims that in one instance when ransom talks proved unsuccessful, Somali captors considered harvesting the crews' organs for sale.

Former UK Foreign Secretary David Miliband has stated that the British government and the international community believe that payments for hostage taking only encourage further hostage taking. However, while incidents of piracy may be encouraged by continuing to pay ransoms, payment of ransoms also ensures that crews who are captured will not be victims of violence leading to death. The rational course may simply be to deal with the problem as it is now understood, rather than to encourage a potentially chaotic evolution. A prohibition on ransoms will not lessen the lure of piracy to Somalis. The existing model has kept people from getting hurt. Refusing to pay ransoms breaks the model and allows pirates to draft the replacement.

Prohibiting ransoms will not lessen incidents of piracy.

Prohibiting ransoms is unlikely to deter pirate attacks. The athletic and logistical difficulty of boarding and capturing vessels at sea will not be increased by a blanket prohibition against payment of ransoms. A ban might only slightly decrease the possibility of a pirate receiving payment for committing such an act. Joseph Cox, president of the Chamber of Shipping America, has lately been working to determine the effects of President [Barack] Obama's newly issued Executive Order 13536, which with some limit, seemingly removes the ability of US ship owners and stakeholders to pay ransoms to Somali pirates if they can be connected to terrorism. Mr. Cox notes that the regulation would apply only after a ship has been pirated, which is too late in the process. "We have to be concerned about preventing [hijackings] from happening."

It is reasonable to think that Somali pirates who have become aware of prohibitions on ransom payments may avoid attacks against ships flagged by those countries, but the pirate's ability to distinguish actual ownership or even the identity of insurers or freight owners by a vessel's flag are scant to none.

Prohibiting ransoms is unlikely to deter pirate attacks.

Jai Sharma, head of the casualty & GA [general average] department of Dolphin Maritime & Aviation Services, notes that pirates might be able to recognize a ship flying the US flag, but due to widespread use of flags of convenience, a US flag ship is a relatively uncommon thing; consequently, it is quite probable that ships controlled by US interests will continue to be taken by pirates. Furthermore, even if the ship is not US controlled, the pirates will not know the identity of the insurers and cargo owners, and therefore will be unable to determine whether these parties are going to be able to contribute to the ransom and associated expenses in general average. Any difficulty in that regard may make the ship owners more reluctant to pay ransoms demanded if contribution from cargo is barred by reason of illegality.

Prohibiting ransoms will increase incidents of violence and terror.

At best, the deterrent aspect of a ransom payment restriction will have only a marginal effect. The decision of a potential pirate to venture to sea for piratical ends will still be based on his few alternatives. As long as legitimate income opportunities for Somalis are limited, it is likely that desperation will continue to drive some to sea for even a remote chance of economic reward.

Due to the complex international relationships in modern shipping, only international legal solidarity against ransom payments would be likely to alter this ransom component of pirate motivations. Even widespread prohibitions against ransom may prove difficult to enforce. Therefore, without significantly decreasing the incentives of pirates to capture vessels and lawlessly disrupt trade, a policy of restricting ransoms will increase incidents of violence and murder of merchant mariners once the Somali model adapts.

Paying Ransoms Is Economical

At the moment ransoms may be an affordable cost of doing business for the shipping industry. Ship owners note that the cost of maintaining armed security, increased insurance premiums, and time and resources consumed debating solutions to threats of piracy may actually exceed costs of simply paying ransoms. Armed security costs Maersk Line Limited more than a million dollars per year for each vessel in the region, and as yet their security has not been required to repel any pirate attacks.

Losses due to delays are another key aspect of economic concern. Crew wages must be paid, as well as costs associated with contracts on the cargo carried, even when the vessel is detained due to hijacking. In addition, protection and indemnity (P&I) insurance covering crew and environmental damages would also increase as the ability to quickly recover the crew and vessel is reduced.

Another major concern of the shipping industry is exposure to liability. Many vessels passing through high-risk waters are now often equipped with weapons. Ship owners are concerned that the legal outcomes of repelling a pirate attack could be worse than simply paying the ransom. There are no international standards for rules of engagement and the issue of liability is unclear regarding the possibility that a mariner injures or kills someone who attacks the ship. [British naval commander Keith] Winstanley points out the likely no-win consequences of either alternative, asking, "Which is worse for the crew, waiting for ransom in an anchored ship, or sitting in a sweltering Pakistani prison?" The IMO [International Maritime Organization] has issued guidance strongly discouraging the use of weapons due to the complexity of staying within the laws of various States, as well as the legal risk of defending against suspected pirates.

The argument that a ban on ransoms may cause ship owners to cease shipping activities, eventually diminishing the target pool and driving pirates into alternative legitimate pursuits, is unconvincing. The slim opportunities for rewarding legitimate work within Somalia, as well as the ever-present need to service ports in the Arabian Sea, make the idea of reduced service extremely speculative. It is more likely that the increased costs required to provide service will be passed through to customers, and other shippers may step in to fill gaps left by those who withdraw from operation in the area.

In addition, a ship owner may not be able to incur the losses of delay as pirates wait for an indefinite period to pressure payment despite the prohibition. Ship owners might have no other option than to wait and hope pirates will release a ship, extending the duration of capture. Head of Dolphin Maritime & Aviation Services' casualty and general average department, Jai Sharma, notes that, "[t]his could go on for a very long time since the pirates do not seem to lack patience and we expect they would be prepared to wait for ages to see whether a ransom can in fact be paid, or whether any suggestion of illegality is simply a negotiating ploy."

A prohibition on the payment of ransoms could be seen as an obstacle to hiring crews for vessels transiting high-risk zones. If crews are not assured they will be reasonably looked after in the event of a hijack, many mariners will be deterred from going to sea. This view would seem to motivate some ship owners to re-route ships until threats from piracy are reduced. However, because the diffuse pool of merchant mariners hails from countries across the globe, it is unlikely that they will effectively organize their unwillingness to sail in these waters. Therefore pressure from merchant mariners is unlikely to affect the maritime industry. Burdening merchant seamen with the task would only result in a massive displacement of mariners who are unwilling or unable to contend with the risks of piracy, only to be replaced with more hardened and perhaps less trained crews.

Finally, if the rules on ransoms are not internationally uniform, States that are permissive of ransom payments will find increased registrations from ship owners whose vessels spend a significant amount of time in high-risk waters. Those States that are prohibitive would likely experience a decline. Evidence of the willingness of ship owners to re-register their vessels' flags has already been seen due to rules permitting the use of armed security.

A prohibition on ransoms will unnaturally distort the economic considerations that shipping stakeholders now consider. Non-uniform international laws on ransoms will increase the complexity and decrease the predictability of resolving hostage outcomes.

The Threat of an Ecological Disaster

To date there have not been any significant incidents involving a pirate-caused ecological disaster. However, it is not difficult to imagine the extensive damage that might be caused in the aftermath of a pirate attack. [Jayant] Abhyankar [deputy director of the Chamber of Commerce's International Maritime Bureau (IMB)] states "The IMB is convinced that, because there will be no second chance with an oil-spill, a pro-active attitude to the possibility is essential and it would be foolhardy to the point of irresponsibility not to take all possible measures to prevent the first one."

Pirates have increased pressure on ransom negotiations by purposefully opening cargo hatches aboard a captured vessel laden with coal—an act that threatened to overheat the cargo. This type of overheating can lead to fire, which might destroy the vessel and cause extensive pollution. Additionally, the difficulty of safely navigating a vessel to an anchorage along the Somali shore could result in accidental grounding and a catastrophic spill.

An ecological disaster is likely to cause immediate and lasting problems as waters and coasts are damaged without easy, effective, or safe means of restoration. Also, the risk of an accidental disaster is likely to increase in accordance with the time a vessel is held in captivity. A prohibition on ransoms removes the possibility of a relatively quick and minimally violent resolution to detainment and increases the threat of ecological disaster caused by dangerous cargo.

Penalizing Ship Owners for Paying Ransoms Is Unfair

Ince & Company International LLP

Ince & Company International LLP is an international law firm based in London.

[Editor's Note: *Shortly after this article was published in March 2010, President Barack Obama issued an Executive Order on Somalia that prohibited payment to key individuals listed in an Annex, which could prevent US indivudals from paying ransoms to pirates, and which has since been in effect for over eighteen months.*]

According to a number of reports in trade press and recent comments from the US State Department, the US administration seems to be flying a kite to test national and industry reaction to an initiative which may use existing UN [United Nations] Resolutions and the US OFAC (Office of Foreign Assets Control) Regulations ("Regulations") to allow them to take action, including the banning of ships involved from US ports, against shipowners who pay ransoms to Somali pirates.

It is difficult to comment in detail because the full scope of the US proposals have not been aired. Indeed, if the reaction is strong enough no formal proposal may be forthcoming. However, our understanding from industry and other sources is that the US is considering having certain pirate leaders named as "designated" people. These may be named at a UN level, using UN Resolution 1844 (on which see below).

Given this approach to ransom payments, it is interesting to note that the High Court in London recently issued a judgment in a case which involved the hijacking of the *Bunga*

Ince & Company International LLP, "Paying Ransoms—Could the US Make This More Difficult?," InceLaw.com, 2011. Copyright © 2011 by Ince & Co. International LLP. All rights reserved. Reproduced by permission.

Melati Dua in 2008. One of the issues was whether the payment of a ransom was contrary to public policy as a matter of English law. It is worth highlighting the words of Mr Justice [David] Steele [of the British high court], where he made it clear that he did not think it right to categorise the payment as contrary to public policy:

> "So far as harm is concerned it is truth that payments of ransom encourage a repetition, the more so if there is insurance cover: the history of Somali piracy is an eloquent demonstration of that. But if the crews of the vessels are to be taken out of harm's way, the only option is to pay the ransom. Diplomatic or military intervention cannot usually be relied upon and failure to pay may put in jeopardy other crews."

Resolution 1844

Resolution 1844, adopted by the Security Council in November 2008, is one of a series of UN Resolutions which deal with the deteriorating situation in Somalia and in general terms implores member states to impose travel bans and to freeze the assets of named individuals and entities who:

1. import weapons into Somalia

2. through their actions, undermine the security and stability of Somalia

3. prevent humanitarian aid from reaching those who it is targeted at in Somalia.

The US will . . . impose sanctions on any entity paying ransoms to [designated pirate leaders].

One key element of the Resolution is that member states are able to nominate such individuals or entities to the relevant Committee established by the UN. In their most recent report in January 2010, the Committee referred to the citing of the Eritrean government by the US, who, it is believed, have previously named three Al Shebah [a Somalia Islamic group with ties to terrorism] commanders, although it is not clear whether those nominations have been accepted by the UN.

It is understood that the US will also be looking to name either individual war lords or groups (perhaps by clan or sub-clan) involved in piracy, on the basis that their actions are undermining and or threatening the stability and security of Somalia. It is believed that the OFAC Regulations could then be used to impose sanctions on any entity paying ransoms to those designated people.

The sanctions could be:

1. the banning from the US of vessels freed from pirates following the payment of ransom

2. the freezing of assets of the shipowners if they have a registered presence in the US.

The difficulties these sanctions could cause for shipowners are compounded by the fact that during the recent collapse of the freight market, many shipowning companies registered a presence to avoid Rule B Attachments in New York. These attachments are a freezing type injunction employed by companies seeking security for claims for litigation in other jurisdictions. The threat of action against companies with offices registered in the US may therefore have some teeth.

It is difficult to understand the rationale behind this move. It appears the motives may be:

1. to persuade the pirates that there is no economic benefit in piracy

2. to force the industry to take greater steps to prevent piracy.

US legislation would not seek to make the payment of a ransom illegal in other countries. Instead it would aim to impose sanctions after the event. There are precedents where the US has imposed sanctions which can interrupt what would otherwise be regarded as normal trade. Cuba is a good example and the shipping sanctions being imposed on shipping companies involved in the delivery of refined petroleum products to Iran show how wide ranging these sanctions can be.

US proposals appear to assume that the pirates approach a hijacking in a rational way. They clearly do not. Even if they became aware of such new law, they would simply assume that if the shipowners could not pay, the fact that they have captured cargo and have shown themselves perfectly happy to wait for months for ransoms to be paid demonstrates a belief that money will eventually be paid from somewhere.

Preventing Piracy

Perhaps a better approach would be to increase the risk to pirates by ensuring that national laws are robust enough to prosecute pirates and would-be pirates. Reports often appear in the press of pirates being captured by naval forces only to be released at a later date without prosecution. It would be better to address this "catch and release" policy before we criminalise the shipowners. Having said that, at the time of writing there have been encouraging reports of the French handing twenty-two recently captured pirates to the Puntland [a region of Somalia] authorities and [of] Kenya sentencing eight others to twenty years in prison. It remains to be seen if this will continue.

One rationale for this initiative could simply be that it is a way to change the shipowners' approach to self-protection. There has been criticism voiced by US Admirals to the effect that shipowners are in the main not adopting Best Management Practice Guidelines and a plaintive cry that shipowners should "do more" to help themselves.

These steps may include having armed guards on board and it appears to be US policy to move towards the arming of US-flagged vessels. Raising the stakes for other shipowners, particularly those with US registered offices or whose vessels regularly call at US ports, through new regulations may pressure them into taking more robust steps to protect their vessels from hijackings, and thus negate the need to pay a ransom. This may clash with the flag state policy or indeed give rise to the other issues, not least [being] the fear that the violence could escalate. Recent events in the Indian Ocean, with reported fire fights between pirates and Spanish fishing trawlers, highlight this fear.

Perhaps a better approach would be to increase the risk to pirates by ensuring that national laws are robust enough to prosecute pirates and would-be pirates.

Problems with US Regulations

Fundamentally it cannot be in anyone's interest to criminalise the victims of a hijacking. The effects of a US move to introduce these Regulations could have serious consequences for those that are affected by piracy, while doing little to address the issue of preventing piracy and dealing with those responsible. The reality is that shipowners are driven by a commercial imperative to free their ships, and, as long as the ransoms remain a minor percentage of the values involved, that will remain the case. Introducing additional hurdles could see the practice of paying ransoms driven underground or elaborate structures being put in place to avoid falling foul of new regulations.

It is interesting that the US is focussing on Somalia alone, notwithstanding the fact that piracy can and does happen elsewhere. Furthermore, this legislation would be specific to shipping and does not address extortion in the wider sense.

The issue is further complicated by the fact that in the US the act of "hostage taking" of a US national overseas is regarded as terrorism under the Patriot Act and knowingly paying money to those involved in terrorism is a criminal act.

Laws attempting to ban ransom payments and indeed freezing assets of families involved have been introduced elsewhere, notably Colombia and Italy, although these too have generated debate. In Colombia these laws were subsequently subject to a Court ruling that allows ransoms where humanitarian factors demand them. Furthermore, these bans were accompanied by the outlawing of kidnap and ransom insurance, which is now a well-established insurance product in the Lloyds [of London insurance firm] market.

The reality is that shipowners are driven by a commercial imperative to free their ships, and, as long as the ransoms remain a minor percentage of the values involved, that will remain the case.

It is therefore difficult to see how the US could take unilateral action against a shipowner without also condemning various insurance companies specialising in this area. Even if such a move was possible it is, of course, made more complicated in shipping in the sense that losses incurred by piracy are a legitimate insured peril and payable under ordinary hull and/or war policies (depending where the risk falls). This then is the real crux of this problem—who pays the ransom and how will the Regulations affect them?

The shipowner may take the lead in any negotiations but ultimately would look to his usual insurer (in the absence of a dedicated kidnap and ransom policy) to pay ship's proportion of the ransom, either as a sue and labour expense or in General Average. If the latter (i.e. when the vessel is laden) then cargo interests (and more likely their insurers) will pay cargo's proportion. Crew, of course, do not contribute to the ransom despite the fact that the threats are essentially made against them.

There are also circumstances (although rare) where the time charterer agrees to bear the cost of a ransom and takes out applicable insurance on the basis that they are bearing the risk of time. Where Time Charters were entered into before the global economic downturn, some of the exposures to losses over a three to four month hijacking are considerable. They can be in excess not only of the final ransom payment, but also of the original, higher demand.

Additional Issues

Even if the legislation singles out the shipowner, questions remain as to exactly who the Regulations would cover. Would they cover the shipowning company, the managers and other ships under management in the same group? What about those companies where the technical management is done by a different third party company? The key issue appears to be the payment of a ransom, in which case what consideration will be given to the cargo interests who may in fact pay a greater proportion of the ransom in certain circumstances? Further how would the Regulations apply to the insurers themselves?

It is difficult to see how the Regulations could be formulated. Putting that aside there is also the very real difficulty of a shipowner knowing exactly to whom he is paying a ransom and whether this person is a nominated individual as per UN guidelines. A shipowner will have done well if during the course of a negotiation he is able to determine which Somalian clan and sub-clan he is dealing with, letting alone identify the individual with whom he is dealing.

Penalising the shipowner, who is but one stakeholder in a maritime venture, would appear not to be the most sensible way to deal with the continued burden of piracy and ransom

demands. The reward side of the equation for pirates continues to rise and although the coalition naval forces appear to
have adopted a more aggressive approach to the issue, there
appears no commensurate increase in risk to a pirate of being
arrested and taken for prosecution. If national governments
want to introduce new policy perhaps that is a better place to
start. Some fifty pirates have been captured in the past week,
thirty five by the French navy. It will be interesting to see
what happens to them.

Appeasement of Pirates Has Never Worked

Joseph Farah

Joseph Farah is a journalist, author, and editor-in-chief of World-NetDaily, a conservative news website.

My how things have changed.

I just heard the US State Department is suggesting we should negotiate with Somali pirates by paying ransom for the release of 26 Bangladeshis on board the hijacked ship *MV Jahan Moni*.

Washington [DC, US government] says "money was the sole objective" behind the hostage-taking, and that the pirates would likely release the captives for far less money than they are demanding because it's the "lean season" for piracy.

Bangladesh has taken a more principled stand—that no nation can pay ransom for piracy.

Next thing you know the U.S. will be contributing to the ransom or paying the whole thing.

This is quite a turnabout in U.S. foreign policy.

The Barbary Pirates

In 1784, Thomas Jefferson, John Adams and Benjamin Franklin were commissioned by the first Congress to assemble in Paris to see about marketing U.S. products in Europe.

Jefferson quickly surmised that the biggest challenge facing U.S. merchant ships were those referred to euphemistically as "Barbary pirates."

They weren't "pirates" at all, in the traditional sense, Jefferson noticed. They didn't drink and chase women, and they re-

Joseph Farah, "'To the Shores of Tripoli . . . ,'" World Net Daily Online, December 27, 2010. www.wnd.com. Copyright © 2010 by WorldNetDaily.com Inc. All rights reserved. Reproduced by permission.

ally weren't out to strike it rich. Instead, their motivation was strictly religious. They bought and sold slaves, to be sure. They looted ships. But they used their booty to buy guns, ships, cannons and ammunition.

Like those we call "terrorists" today, they saw themselves engaged in jihad and called themselves "mujahedeen."

Why did these 18th-century terrorists represent such a grave threat to U.S. merchant ships? With independence from Great Britain, the former colonists lost the protection of the greatest navy in the world. The U.S. had no navy—not a single warship.

Jefferson inquired of his European hosts how they dealt with the problem. He was stunned to find out that France and England both paid tribute to the fiends—who would, in turn, use the money to expand their own armada, buy more weaponry, hijack more commercial ships, enslave more innocent civilians and demand greater ransom.

[Thomas] Jefferson urged the building of a navy to rescue American hostages held [by the Barbary pirates] in North Africa and to deter future attacks on U.S. ships.

This didn't make sense to Jefferson. He recognized the purchase of peace from the Muslims only worked temporarily. They would always find an excuse to break an agreement, blame the Europeans and demand higher tribute.

After three months researching the history of militant Islam, he came up with a very different policy to deal with the terrorists. But he didn't get to implement it until years later.

As the first secretary of state, Jefferson urged the building of a navy to rescue American hostages held in North Africa and to deter future attacks on U.S. ships. In 1792, he commissioned John Paul Jones to go to Algiers under the guise of diplomatic negotiations, but with the real intent of sizing up a future target of a naval attack.

The Problem with Paying Ransoms

Our Western principles hold that each life has value. America was built on the fundamental belief that "all men are created equal . . . with certain inalienable rights . . . [including] life, liberty, and the pursuit of happiness." But when others, who do not share these values, put our lives at risk in the name of money, power, or religion, we are faced with a dilemma. Do we pay the price demanded in order to free those captives, each of whom has value within the context of a free society, and bring relief to their anxious families? Or do we consider the consequences of such an appeasement: that it encourages even more acts of terrorism by proving that our respect for the lives of our people is a valuable bargaining chip; and that the payment of a ransom—money, the release of imprisoned comrades, prestige and power among their peers—is a price we are more than willing to pay in order to save the lives of their hostages.

Appeasement . . . encourages even more acts of terrorism by proving that our respect for the lives of our people is a valuable bargaining chip.

Israel has found that this imbalance in values can elicit dramatic results. When dealing with their enemies, in whose eyes one Israeli life has proven to be worth many of theirs, the exchange of hostages has almost never been equal. Over the last 30 years, Israel has exchanged nearly 7,000 Arab prisoners in order to secure the release of 19 Israelis, and the bodies of eight others. In 2004, for example, Israel traded 436 Arab prisoners and the bodies of 59 Lebanese fighters for one Israeli civilian and the bodies of three Israeli soldiers. In 1996, Israel released 65 prisoners in exchange for the return of the bodies of two soldiers from Lebanon. Israel's largest prisoner ex-

Jefferson was ready to retire a year later when what could only be described as "America's first Sept. 11" happened.

America was struck with its first mega-terror attack by jihadists. In the fall of 1793, the Algerians seized 11 U.S. merchant ships and enslaved more than 100 Americans.

When word of the attack reached New York, the stock market crashed. Voyages were canceled in every major port. Seamen were thrown out of work. Ship suppliers went out of business. What Sept. 11 did to the U.S. economy in 2001, the mass shipjacking of 1793 did to the fledgling U.S. economy in that year.

Accordingly, it took the U.S. Congress only four months to decide to build a fleet of warships.

But even then, Congress didn't choose war, as Jefferson prescribed. Instead, while building what would become the U.S. Navy, Congress sent diplomats to reason with the Algerians. The U.S. ended up paying close to $1 million and giving the pasha of Algiers a new warship, "The Crescent," to win release of 85 surviving American hostages.

Appeasement never works. . . . It's time to learn from history, not repeat its mistakes.

It wasn't until 1801, under the presidency of Jefferson, that the U.S. engaged in what became a four-year war against Tripoli. And it wasn't until 1830, when France occupied Algiers, and later Tunisia and Morocco, that the terrorism on the high seas finally ended.

France didn't leave North Africa until 1962—and it quickly became a major base of terrorism once again.

What's the moral of the story? Appeasement never works. Jefferson saw it. Sept. 11 was hardly the beginning. The war in which we fight today is the longest conflict in human history. It's time to learn from history, not repeat its mistakes.

Let me ask you a simple, common-sense question: Will paying ransom to Muslim pirates end the threat? Or will it more logically help create a new market for piracy—and ensure there is never a "lean season" for it?

Paying Ransoms to Pirates Only Exacerbates Terrorism

Ilana Freedman

Ilana Freedman is CEO and senior analyst for Gerard Group International, a company that provides intelligence analysis for business and homeland security.

Once again a European country has bowed to terrorism and put the rest of the world at heightened risk. On Tuesday, November 17, [2009,] a ransom of $3.3 million was paid by the Spanish government to a pack of Somali pirates, to free the 36 crew members of the Basque tuna seiner fishing boat *Alakrana*. The nature of the small fishing boat made it abundantly clear that the target of this piracy was the human cargo and the high ransom they would command.

The tuna boat was hijacked by pirates in the Indian Ocean before dawn on the morning of October 2. They had cast their nets some 375 miles east of the Somali coast when they were captured. They were held captive for seven weeks while the negotiations between the pirates and the Spanish government dragged on.

It must be a fearful thing to be a fisherman on a boat commandeered by 12 heavily armed pirates who threaten them with death while the weeks of captivity drag on. But the consequences of a government paying a $3 million ransom go far beyond this story. Terrorists are emboldened when they are rewarded for their acts of terror. The potential loss of many more lives than were saved here once again raises the question: where do you draw the line when dealing with terrorism?

Ilana Freedman, "Another Step Backwards for Mankind," www.gerardgroup.com, November 24, 2009. Copyright © 2009 by Gerard Group International. All rights reserved. Reproduced by permission.

change occurred in 1983, when 4,600 Palestinian and Lebanese prisoners were exchanged for six Israeli soldiers captured in Lebanon in 1982.

What Israel has never really learned is that these exchanges prove to terrorists that Israel will always pay a high price for the return of its soldiers and civilians. Gilad Shalit, an Israeli soldier kidnapped into Gaza in a cross-border raid by terrorists, has been held for more than three years. Rumors of his pending release suggest that he will be exchanged for over 100 Palestinians currently in Israeli prisons. [He had not been released as the present volume went to press.]

Among the consequences of these uneven exchanges is that freed terrorists will often return and commit more acts of terror. This incentivizes the capture of Israelis by terrorist organizations like Hamas and Hizballah. In fact, Hamas recently demonstrated this principle, taking it to a new level, when a Gaza 'charity', linked to the terrorist organization, offered $1.4 million to anybody who would capture an Israeli soldier.

Likewise, when it comes to maritime piracy, the ante keeps going up. The alarming rise in piracy in the past year should be a stark warning. A total of 306 incidents were reported to the IMB [International Maritime Bureau] Piracy Reporting Centre (PRC) in the first nine months of this year (in 2008, the total number of attacks for the entire year was 293). In the same period, the use of guns in these attacks has risen by more than 200%. If the pattern continues, the number of attacks on ships plying international waters in 2009 will approach 400.

A total of 661 crewmembers were taken hostage so far this year: 12 kidnapped, seven killed, and eight reported missing. A United Nations Security Council report specifically blamed escalating ransom payments for fuelling the rise of piracy off the Somali coast. Ransom paid in this year alone has exceeded $100 million, making maritime piracy an exceedingly lucrative business. When an adversary is willing to let his own men die as a consequence of achieving a greater aim—whether it be money, religion, or power—he holds the upper hand.

When it comes to maritime piracy, the ante keeps going up. The alarming rise in piracy in the past year should be a stark warning.

Wide-Ranging Consequences

Paying astronomical ransoms to maritime pirates comes at a significant cost, because of the indirect impact on world affairs. First, the cost of shipping rises dramatically, as insurance premiums rise and the cost of goods transported by sea also rise. There is a far more insidious consequence as well, related to the flow of ransom money following payment. The Somali pirates actually see relatively little of the ransom money after the dust settles. They are a small but important link in a much larger organization, whose tendrils reach far into the Middle East and around the world. There, power brokers use the stream of ransom money as a funding mechanism for drugs, money laundering, human trafficking, and terrorism. The same ransom money that returned the hostages to their families, now goes to support suicide bombers and terrorist training. As the appeasement of maritime piracy provides needed capital to fuel these enterprises, its value as a cash cow will spur a piracy epidemic of global proportions.

Piracy Is Terrorism

There is an Arab proverb that says, "He who brings a lion into his home, loses his children to the wild." While the Israelis are willing to trade prisoners for hostages after the fact, they discovered long ago that negotiating with terrorists during an attack is counter-productive and wreaks far more havoc on society than an immediate strong response against the perpetrators. Their longstanding rule against negotiating with terrorists has helped to limit attacks against its population.

The Israeli model has its down-side—because there is always the possibility that innocent hostages from the initial attack may fall as a result of the response. And this is considered a tragedy of epic proportions. But the message is clear and strong, and its practice has saved the lives of countless others.

There are unintended consequences that arise from negotiating with terrorists. Although we think we take the high ground, standing on the lofty principles of fairness and what we consider to be decency, they perceive our kindness as weakness and foolishness. While we negotiate, they laugh at us and plot their next attacks. In the eyes of the terrorist, negotiations are perceived as a sign of weakness and naïveté, giving them time to regroup, and encouraging future attacks. While we seek to appease, they seek out our soft spots at which to aim their weapons. As the Israelis discovered a long time ago, the price of appeasement is far too high to pay.

When we fail to call terrorism by name, we stimulate its growing appetite for violence.

Today, the lion is in our home, and every day it feeds on political correctness and appeasement. When we fail to call terrorism by name, we stimulate its growing appetite for violence. The deaths of thirteen men and women in Fort Hood [Texas, from a serviceman's shooting spree] has demonstrated quite clearly a consequence of our irrational pre-occupation with diversity and political correctness. But we call it murder, not terrorism, and we limit our ability to prosecute it and impede our ability to prevent it from occurring again.

Instead of recognizing deviant behavior for what it is, we try to rationalize why it is normal. Instead of reporting anti-social and violent rhetoric to authorities, we excuse it or ignore it. We try to appease those who would hurt us, and hope that our good intentions will make them magically stop wanting to do us harm.

We cannot afford the luxury of ignoring what is in front of us because it is uncomfortable or politically incorrect. We are at war with an implacable enemy. Whether it takes the form of a pirate on the high seas, an egocentric president in Iran or North Korea, or a jihadist in our backyard, appeasement is the worst possible strategy of all. The $3.3 million ransom paid last week to maritime terrorists will come back to haunt every ship that passes through open waters. Whatever attitude spawned the payment—whether it was fear, cowardice, political correctness, greed, political pressure, compassion, moral blindness, or just fatigue—it is likely to bear the burden of responsibility for setting yet one more precedent for the growth of terrorist empowerment around the world.

Pirates Should Be Confronted Not Paid

Abdon M. Pallasch

Abdon M. Pallasch is a political reporter for the Chicago Sun-Times, *a daily newspaper.*

The United States should push for a ban on ransoms to Somali pirates and let merchant ships arm themselves in the Indian Ocean, Sen. Mark Kirk said Friday [May 6, 2011].

The U.S. might even want to consider putting soldiers on U.S. merchant ships in the area, he said.

The Need to Confront Pirates

Kirk returned this week from a week-long tour of the African coast where the centuries-old scourge of piracy has made an explosive comeback over the past five years.

"This is a problem as old as the sea, and it hadn't been an issue," Kirk said. "Then in 2005, some Somalis went out to warn international fishermen that they were hurting their fishing, and they realized they were the only ones on board with AK-47s and they could demand ransoms."

Kirk flew over pirate-controlled ports on the Somali coast where 23 ships with 483 hostages are anchored. The average ransom being paid has gone from $1.3 million to $5.4 million over the past two years, he said.

The more lucrative cruise ship industry that used to sustain neighboring states such as Kenya has abandoned those waters as the U.S. and other governments have warned citizens to stay out of the pirate-imperiled waters.

Kirk argues it is time for the United States government to make the same decision President Thomas Jefferson did after

Abdon M. Pallasch, "Kirk: U.S. Should Say No to Pirate Ransoms," *Chicago Sun-Times*, May 6, 2011. www.SunTimes.com. Copyright © 2011 by *Chicago Sun-Times*. All rights reserved. Reproduced by permission.

taking office in 1800: It's in the long-term interests of the United States to confront the pirates rather than allowing the ransom culture to grow.

He'll be meeting with Secretary of State Hillary Clinton next week to make that argument in person.

Though no American ships or hostages are involved right now, Americans should care because 70 percent of the world's oil is shipped through these waters, and piracy is increasing the cost of that oil as well as pumping hundreds of millions of dollars into pirate groups he said are allied with [terror network] al-Qaida.

It's in the long-term interests of the United States to confront the pirates rather than allowing the ransom culture to grow.

Kirk asked one of the captured pirate leaders in a Somali prison why he was there.

"Because I captured one too many ships," Kirk said.

A More Aggressive Approach

While the European governments still keep to a policy of paying ransoms for hostages and not attacking the pirates while they hold hostages, other countries such as China, India and Russia more aggressively attack pirated ships, sinking them, then picking up the people left floating in the water to sort pirates from hostages, he said.

Chinese naval captains outlined their strategies for Kirk aboard their ships in the Indian Ocean defending ships that fly the Chinese flag.

The more aggressive approach—refusing to pay ransoms—may pose a threat to the 483 hostages in custody right now, Kirk said, but it's the best long-term strategy to cripple the industry.

"Because we didn't make the tough call in 2008, we went from five hostages in 2008 to 500 today," Kirk said.

Americans should care [about piracy] because 70 percent of world's oil is shipped through these waters, and piracy is increasing the cost of that oil.

South Africa and other countries in the area that serve as refueling and restocking ports prohibit the merchant ships from arming themselves because they don't want to facilitate the arms trade. But Kirk said that leaves the merchant ships defenseless. The U.S. should encourage a policy that allows some token number of guns on a ship—perhaps five—that would allow the ships' crews to defend themselves against pirates.

Chapter 4

How Should the US and Other Nations Combat Pirate Attacks?

Chapter Preface

Most people think of piracy as an attack on ships at sea, but there is no single legal definition of piracy that has been agreed upon by all nations around the globe. Instead, there are various definitions provided in international treaties and used by various nations. Defining piracy is important for cataloging the number of piracy incidents and understanding the growing problem of piracy, and the lack of a clear definition, many commentators say, makes it difficult for piracy crimes to be prosecuted.

The main international law applicable to piracy is the 1982 United Nations Convention on the Law of the Sea (UNCLOS), a treaty that came into force in 1994 and that has been ratified by almost every country in the world (except for the United States). UNCLOS sets forth the rights and responsibilities of nations in their use of the world's oceans, in order to protect the ocean environment and manage marine resources. It also, however, deals with acts of piracy. In Article 101 of UNCLOS, piracy is defined as:

(a) any illegal acts of violence or detention, or any act of depredation, committed for private ends by the crew or the passengers of a private ship or a private aircraft, and directed:

(i) on the high seas, against another ship or aircraft, or against persons or property on board such a ship or aircraft;

(ii) against a ship, aircraft, persons or property in a place outside the jurisdiction of any state;

(b) any act of voluntary participation in the operation of a ship or of an aircraft with knowledge of facts making it a pirate ship or aircraft;

(c) any act of inciting or of intentionally facilitating an act described in subparagraph (a) or (b).

UNCLOS gives all nations the right to use their warships to seize pirate ships and prosecute pirates.

However, UNCLOS has one significant weakness—it only applies to acts of piracy on the high seas. This means acts of maritime violence and detention that are committed within a country's territorial waters—generally considered to be the twelve miles from the coastline—are not considered to be piracy by international law. In most areas of the world, this is not a problem because almost all countries police their own territorial waters and prevent acts of piracy in these waters. The UNCLOS weakness becomes very important, however, in coastal waters near poor and politically weak nations that either cannot or will not hunt down pirates operating in their jurisdiction.

The most glaring example of this phenomenon is the rapidly rising number of pirate attacks off the coast of Somalia, a very unstable country in North Africa that is simply not able to fund or operate a coast guard capable of cracking down on Somali pirates. This has created a haven for piracy in Somalia's waters, and not surprisingly, piracy has flourished there in recent years.

In June 2008, however, the Security Council, the governing body of the United Nations (UN), tried to address this weakness in the UNCLOS treaty by adopting a resolution authorizing shipping nations to act against piracy within the territorial waters of Somalia. Specifically, UN Resolution 1816 authorized the international naval force patrolling the region to enter Somalia's waters and to take all means necessary to repress acts of piracy there. This has been understood to mean that military action can be taken against pirates in Somali waters, and several other UN resolutions have strengthened this authority to allow pirates to be pursued even onto dry land in Somalia, where pirates find sanctuary. But despite these UN resolutions, piracy has continued to flourish near Somalia, largely because pirates simply have changed their tactics to avoid capture. Today, instead of restricting attacks to Somalia's territorial waters, pirates operate over a broad range of ocean, making them much harder to locate and catch. In addition, nations have been reluctant to use military force, such as missile strikes, in Somalia, largely because of concern for civilian casualties.

Additional definitional problems and obstacles concerning piracy involve whether pirates are considered to be criminals or military prisoners of war. Traditionally, they were considered both, which meant they could either be killed or be captured and tried, whichever was more convenient for the country whose ships were being attacked. Under modern international law, however, pirates can no longer be treated militarily as enemy combatants (that is, attacked and killed), so ships must try to capture them instead. And once captured, many legal scholars argue that pirates must be accorded criminal rights as well as humanitarian treatment under the Geneva Conventions, treaties that set the international standards for prisoners of war. This means that pirate ships cannot legally be seized and pirates cannot be forcefully dealt with except in self defense—that is, unless they are actually in the process of attacking and boarding another ship.

Prosecuting pirates presents still other difficulties. Besides the cost of detaining and mounting a prosecution against captured pirates, there are additional procedural issues. These include, for example, providing counsel and translation services to pirate defendants, as well as arranging for and transporting prosecution witnesses for trials and taking care not to violate the religious scruples of Somalis, who are often Muslim. In addition, there is no internationally agreed-upon forum for trying pirate defendants. Somalia clearly has no adequate legal system to do so, and although nearby countries such as Kenya have agreed to help with prosecuting Somali pirates, prosecuting in a foreign country is difficult.

Even in the best of circumstances, the prosecution of pirates is a thorny endeavor. The US military, for example, has detained a number of individuals accused of acts of piracy against US ships, and the United States has prosecuted two cases in US federal courts, with differing results. The pirate defendants in these cases were caught in the act of piracy and captured by the US Navy, then sent to Norfolk, Virginia, for criminal trials in the US District Court for the Eastern District of Virginia. In one case, the defendants were found guilty of piracy as well as other charges, but the second case is being appealed by the prosecution after the court dismissed the charge of piracy, finding that there was no actual robbery at sea—the US Supreme Court's definition of piracy. The viewpoints in this chapter address the question of prosecution and other measures that have been proposed to combat piracy.

Multiple Approaches Must Be Taken to Manage the Piracy Problem

Andrew J. Shapiro

Andrew J. Shapiro is assistant secretary of state for the Bureau of Political-Military Affairs, a federal agency within the US Department of State that provides policy direction to the Department of Defense in the areas of international security, security assistance, military operations, defense strategy and plans, and defense trade.

Piracy is an age old problem. Pirates in the Mediterranean plagued the Roman Republic. In the sixteenth and seventeenth century piracy bedeviled European merchant ships in the Caribbean and elsewhere. America, too, confronted piracy in its earliest days. In the late eighteenth and early nineteenth centuries, U.S. merchant ships and crews were subject to routine attacks by pirates from the Barbary States of North Africa. For years, it was deemed cheaper to pay them off than to fight. Then, as now, this answer proved counterproductive and unsustainable. The United States intensified its military and diplomatic efforts, eventually ending the tribute payments to Barbary pirates in 1815. The problem of how to deal with rogue individuals determined to exploit the security weaknesses in commercial maritime trade is not a new problem.

Yet the modern day implications of piracy are now global in scope. In today's globalized age the problem of piracy is one that affects not just individual countries or shipping companies but potentially the entire global economy. We live in an era of complex and integrated global supply chains where

Andrew J. Shapiro, "US Approaches to Counter-Piracy," Remarks of Andrew J. Shapiro, Assistant Secretary, Bureau of Political-Military Affairs, to International Institute for Strategic Studies, Washington, DC, March 30, 2011. State.gov. Copyright © 2011 by US Department of State. All rights reserved. Reproduced by permission.

people in countries around the world depend on safe and reliable shipping lanes for their food, their energy, their medicine, and basic consumer goods. By threatening one of the world's busiest shipping lanes, piracy off the Horn of Africa threatens not just specific ships, but has broader strategic implications.

The problem is both significant and urgent.

By threatening one of the world's busiest shipping lanes, piracy off the Horn of Africa threatens not just specific ships, but has broader strategic implications.

Piracy Is Getting Worse

Despite two years of international political and naval coordination, the problem is growing worse. Last year, 2010, witnessed the highest number of successful pirate attacks and hostages taken on record. And thus far 2011 is on track to be even higher. Close to 600 mariners from around the world are being held hostage in the region, some for as long as six months. Tragically, four Americans were brutally murdered by Somali pirates just last month [February 2011].

The attacks are more ruthless, more violent and wider ranging. Hostages have been tortured and used as human shields and blowtorches have been used to open safe haven areas on ships in order to seize crews, and hold them for ransom. Pirates currently hold around 30 ships, most for ransom.

As international action has been taken to address the challenge, the pirates have responded. The way pirates operate has become more sophisticated. In recent months the use of mother ships—which are themselves pirated ships with hostage crews—has extended the pirates' reach far beyond the Somali Basin. Mother ships launch and re-supply groups of pirates who use smaller, faster boats for attacks. They can carry dozens of pirates and tow many skiffs for multiple simultaneous attacks.

This has made pirates more difficult to interdict and more effective at operating in seasonal monsoons that previously restricted their activities. Somali pirates now operate in a total sea space of approximately 2.5 million square nautical miles, an increase from approximately 1 million square nautical miles two years ago. This increase makes it difficult for naval or law enforcement ships and other assets to reach the scene of a pirate attack quickly enough to disrupt an ongoing attack.

Counter-Piracy Efforts

At Secretary [Hillary] Clinton's direction, we are intensively reviewing our counter-piracy efforts to determine an even more energetic and comprehensive approach to respond to piracy in the Arabian Sea, Gulf of Aden, and the Indian Ocean region. As we move forward, we are looking into many additional possible courses of action that seek to overcome the ongoing challenges of piracy.

In the near and mid-term, we plan to focus on several approaches that have the potential to significantly increase risks to the pirates while reducing by equal measure any potential rewards that they think they may gain. We are considering a broad range of options, from intensifying naval operations, to pursuing innovative approaches to prosecute and incarcerate pirates through innovative national and international approaches. Furthermore, we are looking at additional ways to more aggressively target those who organize, lead, and profit from piracy operations, including disrupting the financial networks that support them.

But before I go into depth on our way forward, let me discuss briefly the actions that are already under way.

To address the problem, the United States has, from the beginning, adopted a multilateral approach. Piracy affects the international community as a whole and can only be effectively addressed through broad, coordinated, and comprehensive international efforts. In January 2009, we helped establish the Contact Group on Piracy off the Coast of Somalia, which now includes over 60 nations as well as international and industry organizations, to help coordinate national and international counter-piracy policies and actions.

We have also developed an integrated multi-dimensional approach toward combating piracy that focuses on: security—through the projection of military power to defend commercial and private vessels; prevention—through best practices measures conducted by the private sector; and deterrence—through effective legal prosecution and incarceration. . . .

Achieving stability and good governance in Somalia represents the only sustainable long-term solution to piracy.

This multi-dimensional approach, focusing on security by expanding naval activities, emphasizing prevention through encouraging best practice measures by the private sector, and providing a deterrent through legal prosecution, provides a solid framework for our counter-piracy efforts.

Unfortunately further action is needed. As pirates have adapted their tactics to evade naval counter-piracy operations and shippers' reliance on best management practices, we must respond in-kind by re-energizing and refocusing our counter-piracy approach. We are dealing with smart, hardened criminals who adapt to changing situations. We need to adapt to and counter their actions while moving forward with the sense of urgency the situation demands.

Before I continue, it is important to recognize that piracy's root cause is state failure in Somalia, and cannot be resolved exclusively through naval patrols and interdictions. The reality is that there will be no end to piracy at sea until there is both political reconciliation and economic recovery on the ground in Somalia and a local government capable of and willing to enforce law and order on land and offshore. Achieving stability and good governance in Somalia represents the only sustainable long-term solution to piracy.

We are currently pursuing a diplomatic dual-track approach in Somalia to support the most important lines of action for countering piracy: building governance, security, and economic livelihoods on land in Somalia. On track one, we continue to support the Transitional Federal Government and the Djibouti Peace Process, as well as the African Union Mission in Somalia.

On track two, we are expanding engagement with local and regional administrations, civil society groups, and Somali clan leaders outside the Djibouti Peace Process who seek stability in Somalia and oppose extremism, including those in Somaliland, Puntland, and parts of South Central Somalia. In coordination with international partners, we will evaluate the utility of increased partnerships with regional governments of Somaliland and Puntland, as well as with local and regional administrative units throughout South Central Somalia, who are opposed to and who are willing to address piracy and governance concerns.

Achieving the necessary governance improvement throughout Somalia will not happen overnight, but this cannot deter us from supporting every improvement we can for the sake of greater stability in Somalia and, in the process, combating piracy.

Acknowledging the challenge of the situation ashore does not preclude progress at sea. We can make advances in combating piracy, irrespective of the situation in Somalia. But we must understand that this is a problem without a simple solution. There exists no silver bullet to solve modern piracy, instead, there are a number of measures that can be taken to manage the problem and reduce its impact.

In the near and mid-term we can focus on several approaches that have the potential to significantly increase risks to the pirates while at the same time reduce their potential rewards. We are considering a broad range of options. These center on four key areas: pursuing additional mechanisms to prosecute and incarcerate pirates: aggressively targeting those who organize, lead, and profit from piracy operations; exploring expanded military options that will not place undue risks or burdens on our armed forces; and intensifying efforts to encourage the shipping industry to employ best management practices.

There exists no silver bullet to solve modern piracy, instead, there are a number of measures that can be taken to manage the problem and reduce its impact.

Prosecution and Incarceration

First, on enhancing the prosecution and incarceration of pirates. One of our major efforts to counter piracy has been to find creative ways to increase the ability and willingness of other states to undertake what should be a national responsibility to hold criminals accountable for attacks on national interests. The United States has actively prosecuted pirates involved in attacks on U.S. vessels where there has been sufficient evidence to support the case. To date, that totals 26 persons involved in several attacks:

- the April 2009 attack on the MAERSK ALABAMA,

- attacks in April of last year on the USS NICHOLAS and the USS ASHLAND,

- and most recently, the attack in February that resulted in the killing of the four Americans on the QUEST.

Fourteen men, thirteen from Somalia and one from Yemen, have been indicted on federal criminal charges for their suspected involvement in this heinous incident. The Somali pirate convicted in the MAERSK ALABAMA attack received a sentence of 33 years and 9 months and the pirates involved in the NICHOLAS attack have received life sentences plus 80 years. These successful prosecutions, like the over 900 other national prosecutions taking place around the world, prove that pirates can be successfully prosecuted in any state with the basic judicial capacity and political will to do so.

Despite these successes, we need to acknowledge the reality that many states, to varying degrees, have not demonstrated sustained political will to criminalize piracy under their domestic law and use such laws to prosecute those who attack their interests and incarcerate the convicted. The world's largest flag registries—so-called "flags of convenience"—have proven either incapable or unwilling to take responsibility. And given the limited venues for prosecution, states have been reluctant to pursue prosecutions of apparent or incomplete acts of piracy, limiting our ability to prosecute suspects not caught in the middle of an attack.

One of the most important things we must do is expand incarceration capacity in the region, as lack of prison capacity is perhaps the most common reason states are reluctant to accept pirates for prosecution.

It is true that suspected pirates have been successfully prosecuted in ordinary courts throughout history. Because of this, the [Barack Obama] Administration has previously been reluctant to support the idea of creating an extraordinary international prosecution mechanism for this common crime. Instead, the Administration has focused on encouraging regional states to prosecute pirates domestically in their national courts. However, in light of the problems I've described to you today, the United States is now willing to consider pursuing some creative and innovative ways to go beyond ordinary national prosecutions and enhance our ability to prosecute and incarcerate pirates in a timely and cost-effective manner. We are working actively with our partners in the international community to help set the conditions for expanded options in the region. In fact, we recently put forward a joint proposal with the United Kingdom suggesting concrete steps to address some of the key challenges we continue to face.

One of the most important things we must do is expand incarceration capacity in the region, as lack of prison capacity is perhaps the most common reason states are reluctant to accept pirates for prosecution. We are already seeing progress in this area. Just this week, a new maximum security prison opened in Northern Somalia to hold convicted pirates. We also support the efforts under way to develop a framework to accommodate the transfer of convicted pirates back to Somalia to serve their sentences in their home country.

In addition, we have suggested consideration of a specialized piracy court or chamber to be established in one or more regional states. The international community is currently considering this idea, along with similar models that would combine international and domestic elements. These ideas are under discussion both in the UN Security Council and in the Contact Group.

It is also critical to continue to support and enhance the prosecution-related programs in the region that are already under way. And we continue to believe one of the most vital aspects remains Somalia's long term ability to construct its own active and independent judicial system.

Targeting Financial Flows

The second area we are considering is how to more effectively target financial flows from piracy, possibly by using approaches similar to the ones we use to target terrorists.

Somali piracy is an organized criminal enterprise, like a mafia or racketeering criminal organization. A key element of our overall counter-piracy approach is the disruption of piracy-related financial flows. We need to hit pirate supply lines—cutting them off at the source. A significant effort must be made to track where pirates get their fuel, supplies, ladders and outboard motors in Somalia and in other nearby countries and to explore means to disrupt this supply. Most importantly, we must focus on pirate leaders and financiers to deny them the means to benefit from ransom proceeds. They must be tracked and hunted by following the money that fuels their operations using all available information. This should include tracing the money that fuels their operations with the same level of rigor and discipline we currently employ to combat other transnational organized crime.

This is particularly critical, considering the recent uncorroborated open source reports of possible links, direct or indirect, between al-Shabaab [a Somali Islamic group with ties to terrorists] in Somalia—specifically al-Shabaab-linked militia—and pirates. Al-Shabaab and the pirates operate largely in separate geographic areas and have drastically opposed ideologies. However, we have seen reports that al-Shabaab is receiving ad-hoc protection fees from pirate gangs working in the same area. Obviously, this is concerning. Let me be clear: while we have seen no evidence to date of direct ties between the two groups, it would not be uncommon for criminal gangs working in the same ungoverned space to share resources or pay kickbacks to one another.

Finally, it is time to explore additional means to map and disrupt the financial flows and criminal masterminds behind the business of piracy before any links are solidified or money is put into the pockets of a group responsible for terrorist attacks. At the beginning of March [2011], the United States hosted a meeting of Contact Group members at which the international community began discussing the development of methods to detect, track, disrupt, and interdict illicit financial transactions connected to piracy and the criminal networks that finance piracy. As we make progress and pirate leaders are identified, we should press local authorities in the piracy-affected region to take action against these leaders and either prosecute them or turn them over to other states for prosecution. Piracy is impacting Americans', Africans', and others' lives around the world, and we should devote resources commensurate to the problem.

A key element of our overall counter-piracy approach is the disruption of piracy-related financial flows.

Military Measures

The third area we are exploring for increased action involves additional ways to work with our Department of Defense [DoD] colleagues to take further action at sea, focusing on steps that would have real impacts on pirate activity without overextending our military. For its part, the United States Navy is already taking proactive measures to remove pirate boats from action when they can do so without unduly risking human life or unnecessarily expending scarce resources. Just last week, U.S. naval forces successfully answered a Philippine-flagged merchant vessel's distress call as pirates attempted to board. U.S. forces, already in the area as part of Operation Enduring Freedom, fired warning shots, causing the pirates to flee and foiling the attack. As American assets were already on the scene, the U.S. military was ready and able to respond without stretching our armed forces too thin.

We at the State Department need to continue to work with our DoD colleagues to explore using other tools at our disposal to further disrupt pirate vessels at sea. Of course, we must always act in a fashion that does not cause the situation on land in Somalia to worsen.

Fourth and finally, we must intensify our efforts to encourage commercial vessels to adopt best management practices. The best defense against piracy is vigilance on the part of the maritime industry. The vast majority of successful pirate attacks are against ships that do not adopt best management practices. The U.S. government requires U.S.-flagged vessels sailing in designated high-risk waters to take additional security measures, including having extra lookouts, having extra communications equipment, and being prepared at all times to evade or resist pirate boarding. I would note that, to date, not a single ship employing armed guards has been successfully pirated.

Combating piracy is not just the job of governments. It requires joint action from both the international community and the private sector. If all commercial fleets worldwide were to implement the measures as appropriate, we would be in a much better position to reduce the rate of successful pirate attacks. Our partners in the maritime industry must continue to step up and take further action to do their part.

In the cat and mouse game of modern day piracy, we must always look for new methods and new approaches to improve our efforts. After all, this is exactly what the pirates are doing. I believe we have the right multi-faceted framework in place to address the challenge. Focusing on security by expanding naval activities; emphasizing prevention by encouraging best practice measures by the private sector and dissuading lavish ransom sums; providing a deterrent through enhanced legal prosecution; and efforts to disrupt the financial flows all provide a solid way forward. There is much work to do in the coming months and years, but through the shared commitment of the United States and the international community the challenge of modern day piracy is one that we will surely meet.

Shipping Nations Should Coordinate Efforts to Prosecute Pirates

James Kraska and Brian Wilson

James Kraska teaches at the Naval War College and previously was oceans policy adviser for the Joint Chiefs of Staff. Brian Wilson is a senior navy lawyer in Washington, DC, and earlier worked as oceans policy adviser in the Office of the Undersecretary of Defense for Policy.

The seizure by Somali pirates on September 25, 2008, of the *Faina*, a Ukrainian-flagged vessel transporting 33 Russian tanks and depleted uranium ammunition to Kenya for consignment delivery to the Sudan People's Liberation Army was startling in its audacity and haul. Even more alarming, however, was the November hijacking of the 1,000-foot super-tanker *Sirius Star*. The Liberian-flagged vessel, owned by Saudi Arabia's Aramco, was carrying more than $100 million in oil to the United States when pirates seized the ship and its 25 crew members some 400 miles out to sea, then motored for the Somali coast and dropped anchor. Admiral Michael Mullen, chairman of the Joint Chiefs of Staff, was stunned by the capture, which sent shocks through global energy markets. The seizure of a supertanker was unprecedented, and the daring attack so far from shore suggested the pirates were using the shipping industry's open-access automatic identification system to intercept merchant ships. Merchant ships on international voyages are required to transmit locational data, but criminal gangs at sea operating commercial equipment can receive these signals as easily as do naval forces and maritime law enforcement—and use it to target ships. Since January

James Kraska and Brian Wilson, "Combatting Piracy in International Waters," *World Policy Journal*, February 23, 2011. www.worldpolicy.org. Copyright © 2011 by World Policy Institute. All rights reserved. Reproduced by permission.

[2011], more than 97 ships have been hijacked in the dangerous waters off Somalia and Yemen, and the ransom for some vessels can fetch into the millions of dollars.

Maritime piracy is experiencing a renaissance not seen since the period of the Barbary pirates. Instability from maritime piracy in the Gulf of Aden is sending ripples throughout the global supply chain, which is already reeling from the collapse of shipping rates brought on by the worldwide economic slowdown. The Baltic Dry Index, which measures the cost of shipping most commodities other than oil, has plummeted to its lowest level in six years and has fallen 93 percent from its peak in May 2008. Indeed, the surge in piracy is coming at the worst time for the shipping industry. More problematic, the resurgence is occurring along critical sea lanes: 20,000 ships pass through the Gulf of Aden adjacent to the Indian Ocean each year, transporting cargo that includes 12 percent of the world's daily oil supply.

While it is impossible to eradicate maritime piracy completely, the threat can be greatly reduced if we broaden efforts to work with international partners. Significantly reducing criminal acts at sea in an area that stretches the distance from Miami to Maine, however, poses significant logistical, operational, and political challenges which require us to work smarter, not harder. This means that although there have been greater calls for expanded naval patrols in the western Indian Ocean, these efforts will not be effective until we change the way we address the problem. What is needed now is a network of shipping states, regional partners, and major maritime powers that can collaborate on how to respond to piracy attacks.

Piracy Is Out of Control

Piracy in the Gulf of Aden is "out of control," reports Captain Pottengal Mukundan, director of the International Maritime Bureau. The area is the unfortunate home to the highest risk of maritime piracy in the world. To counter the threat, nations for the first time have begun to employ maritime power in the Horn of Africa. Warships from NATO [North Atlantic Treaty Organization] and the European Union have deployed to the Gulf of Aden to conduct patrols or participate in the multinational Combined Task Force 150. Naval forces from the United Kingdom, Canada, Turkey, Germany, Denmark, the Netherlands, France, Pakistan, India, Iran, Russia, and other countries have also deployed to the area. Furthermore, the private military security contractor Blackwater has made available to commercial shippers in the Gulf of Aden the services of a security escort ship that includes a helicopter, as an organic naval aviation capability is essential for ships to conduct effective maritime security operations. Although the vessel will not be armed, it will carry armed security personnel who can operate from rigid hull inflatable boats.

While it is impossible to eradicate maritime piracy completely, the threat can be greatly reduced if we broaden efforts to work with international partners.

These patrols have had limited success. In November [2010], Russia, Britain, and India separately thwarted multiple piracy attacks. During the summer and fall of 2008, the U.S. Fifth Fleet and an associated coalition task force repelled two dozen pirate attacks. But for every success there are many attacks that go undeterred, and the pirates have only become bolder. Because of the vast geographic swath—2.5 million square miles—naval forces are simply unable to prevent most attacks. Moreover, once pirates successfully board and hijack a ship, they take the crew hostage and threaten to sink the vessel, limiting options by on-scene warships to rescue the crew and free the boat. Incredibly, nearly 600 seafarers were taken hostage in 2008 and 250 of them and dozens of ships are still being held for ransom by pirates in the area of Harardhere,

Somalia. The situation is reminiscent of the Barbary pirates who terrorized the Mediterranean Sea from the seventeenth to the nineteenth centuries, seizing vessels, cargo, and hostages from European and American ships, and exacting ransom and tribute from governments and private individuals. Vice Admiral William E. Gortney, commander of the U.S. Fifth Fleet which plies the waters of the Arabian Gulf and Horn of Africa, notes that coalition warships patrolling the Gulf of Aden have been so frustrated by piracy attacks against merchant shipping that commercial vessels will have to assume that, if attacked, they are on their own. After *Sirius Star* was seized, Odfjell, a leading Norwegian shipping group, suspended transits through the area due to concerns over safety. Danish shipper Maersk, one of the world's largest, is considering forgoing the Suez Canal and routing ships around the Cape of Good Hope in order to avoid piracy-prone Somalia. In either case, the cost of shipping and the time of transit—an additional two weeks at sea—would increase greatly.

In 2006, the British Parliament concluded that the growth in piracy over the past decade represents an "appalling amount of violence against the maritime community." Maritime piracy, which includes hostage-taking or kidnapping, even murder, imposes human and economic costs on shippers which deter legitimate marine commerce upon which our economies so deeply depend. In the Indian and Pacific Oceans, maritime piracy costs shipping companies some $13–$15 billion annually in losses. In recent months, insurance rates have soared. Premiums for a single transit through the Gulf of Aden, for example, have risen from $500 to as much as $20,000. Beyond the immediate threat to crews, property, and ships, maritime piracy endangers sea lines of communication, interferes with freedom of navigation and the free flow of commerce, and undermines regional stability. Piracy also is corrosive to political and social development in Africa, interrupting capital formation and economic development, abetting corruption, and empowering private armies. Left unchecked, the cumulative effect of piracy eventually can lead to the decline of vibrant commercial centers. In the late sixteenth century, for example, piracy from Algerian and Tunisian corsairs triggered an irreversible decline in the viability of Venice as a trading city state. Today, burgeoning piracy off the coast of East Africa is imperiling mariners, weakening the global shipping industry, and has the potential to disrupt the flow of oil to the world economy. . . .

The Prison Problem

A tremendously difficult problem naval powers face with piracy is not a lack of operational resources to counter the threat, but what to do with the perpetrators once caught. Once pirates are detained and become "persons under control," there are currently no good options. What does the dog do when it catches the car? Determining which state should prosecute pirates seized at sea is particularly vexing. It is typical of the vessels attacked by Somali pirates that the ship may be registered in one nation, such as Greece, owned by a corporation located in another nation, such as South Korea, and operated by a crew comprised of nationals of several additional countries, such as the Philippines and Pakistan. Furthermore, the vessel is likely to be transporting either containerized cargo or bulk commodities owned by companies in another country, and the piracy attack may have been interrupted by a warship from yet another nation.

Although any country may assert jurisdiction in the case of a universal crime, each has a special interest in the outcome of the prosecution. On the high seas—or in any other place outside the jurisdiction of an individual country, such as a poorly governed area like Somalia's territorial seas—any nation may take action against piracy. Pirated ships may be boarded, pirates detained, and the property on board the vessel seized and submitted to admiralty and criminal courts.

Only warships, military aircraft, or vessels in government service, however, may exercise this authority.

Boarding hijacked vessels or pirate ships may be conducted under a variety of legal rationales. First, the flag state in which the vessel is registered may authorize a boarding by its own authorities or another state. Second, since piracy, along with slavery, is a universal crime, every nation may seize a pirated ship. In such cases, naval forces may exercise the right of visit if there are reasonable grounds to believe a ship is engaged in piracy. Third, all nations are entitled to exercise the inherent right of individual and collective self-defense, as set forth in the UN [United Nations] Charter. Typically, international law would permit several nations to act against piracy, including the state of registry or flag of the attacked vessel, the nationality of any of the crew members, and in some cases, coastal and port states in the region.

But none of these are great options because it takes awhile to sort out the logistical and legal issues. Captured pirates cannot be turned over to local authorities in Somalia—because, in many cases, there are no responsible local authorities in that failed state. Moreover, some tribal regions might either let the pirates go or impose excessive, disproportionate punishments under tribal justice or Islamic law. Likewise, the great expense and logistical and legal burdens of transporting the pirates to a Western country for prosecution are daunting.

On the high seas . . . any nation may take action against piracy. Pirated ships may be boarded, pirates detained, and the property on board the vessel seized.

Achieving Stability in Somalia

Any long-term solution to the region's piracy threat requires addressing lawlessness in Somalia. Of course, the very best option would be to have a stable, responsible, and moderate government in Mogadishu that could rein in the maritime pirate gangs operating along the coast. Somalia was thrown into chaos in 1992, and except for a brief rule by an Islamic government in 2006, the country has teetered on anarchy. The Transitional Federal Government (TFG) is the most significant authority in the country, but it is composed of a few leaders presiding over a state apparatus that is an empty shell, feckless, ineffective, and lacking in the core capabilities necessary to run a state. The ability to deal successfully with Somalia's maritime pirates would improve if the country is stabilized under a responsible government. But even then, international collaboration would be critical to resolving the problem because the drama includes ships, people, cargoes, and crews from around the world. Thus, taking the fight to the pirates demands a collaborative legal and operational approach.

The state that ships are registered under, known as "flag states," are often countries with open registries but few judicial and logistical resources. Panama or Liberia, for instance, may have limited capacities to prosecute. In 2006, these difficulties required the United States to provide temporary custody for Somali pirates on board U.S. warships. One example: after the United States declined to prosecute suspected pirates who had fired on a U.S. Navy warship on March 18, 2006, it took several months to repatriate completely all 12 Somalis, some of whom had significant injuries and required considerable medical treatment. The suspected pirates resided, for the most part, on U.S. warships during the period from capture to repatriation. But warships no longer have functional brig facilities, so keeping pirates on board naval vessels presents security challenges within the ship. These difficulties with captured pirates are the reason several countries have returned them to the beach without taking any legal action. The British Foreign Ministry has told the Royal Navy that pirates brought into the country for prosecution could be granted political asylum. In September 2008, the Danish Navy released ten captured pirates on the beach because jurisdiction in the case was unclear and Somalia lacked the capacity to take them to court. This approach has been criticized as "catch and release." That said, France has twice in 2008 successfully interdicted Somali pirates and brought them to Paris to stand trial, and Kenya has stepped forward to prosecute pirates captured by British and American forces.

Although it is always preferable to work through regional nations to conduct piracy prosecutions, the countries on Africa's east coast have nascent legal systems and are notoriously lacking in resources for law enforcement and the judiciary. Thus, while piracy is a universal crime, states that lack vessels and aircraft to patrol their coastal zone or the legal infrastructure to bring pirates to justice are not able to play a constructive role in solving the crisis.

Effective action against piracy requires immediate action to develop policy frameworks and legal capacity of these states. The USS *Churchill* incident is a useful case in point. In January 2006, an Indian dhow, the *Delta Ranger*, was overtaken in international waters by Somali pirates armed with rocket-propelled grenades and AK-47 assault rifles. The *Churchill* was in the vicinity; it seized control of the vessel and detained the pirates. After desperately trying to find a nation willing to assert jurisdiction over the pirates, Kenya finally stepped forward. The pirates were tried in a court in Mombasa and later convicted and sentenced to prison for seven years. This was a noteworthy example of effective police and legal action. Replicating this success should be the international community's focus. Currently, however, each case is addressed in ad hoc fashion. There is no mechanism to untangle the diplomatic and logistical knot.

An International Effort

Coordination, not kinetic action aimed at sinking pirate mother ships and destroying coastal havens, will solve the piracy problem. In other words, piracy will not fade until effective deterrents—namely prosecution and punishment—are in place. And with Somalia unable to provide such deterrents, it falls to the international community to make progress in this area. Maritime piracy is a violation of international law and a universal crime that imposes a duty on all states to take action. The United Nations Convention on the Law of the Sea, the constitution for the world's oceans, defines maritime piracy as an illegal act of violence or detention committed for private ends. This is distinguished from maritime terrorism, which is committed for political ends. While any country may lawfully act to suppress maritime piracy, only major maritime powers that operate "blue water" fleets with naval aviation have the capability to patrol sea lanes for long periods.

Developing the modern legal capacity and frameworks in international law necessary to defeat piracy begins at the International Maritime Organization (IMO) in London. The IMO is the specialized UN agency for maritime matters and has 167 member states. Because the organization is technical rather than political, and operates under consensus decision-making rules, it has served as an effective, no-nonsense venue for making shipping safer and more secure. In 2005, the IMO adopted a resolution that strongly urged nations to take legislative, judicial, and law enforcement action to receive and prosecute or extradite pirates arrested by warships or other government vessels and to continue consultations by which technical assistance can be brought to regional states to enhance their capacity for repressing piracy. Addressing the problem of piracy off the coast of Somalia, in November 2007 the IMO adopted another resolution that called on regional states in East Africa to conclude an international agreement to prevent, deter, and suppress piracy. This resolution provides valuable momentum for the effort within the capitals of East Africa and among the major shipping registry nations such as Malta and Liberia, all states which generally avoid getting out in front of global politics.

Last summer [2010], at the prompting of the IMO, the UN Security Council turned its attention toward combating piracy, calling on flag, port, and coastal states of the victims and perpetrators of piracy to cooperate extensively in counter-piracy actions off the Somali coast. In particular, the resolution suggested nations should cooperate in determining jurisdictional issues, and work together in the investigation and prosecution of pirates. It is especially important that, once a piracy attack is disrupted at sea, states coordinate to provide real-time disposition and logistics assistance with respect to the suspected pirates, victims, and witnesses. The Security Council resolution does not compel a state to accept suspected pirates, victims, or witnesses from a warship, but it provides an umbrella of political legitimacy that should make it easier to participate in collective action.

Piracy will not fade until effective deterrents—namely prosecution and punishment—are in place. And ... [this task] falls to the international community.

The Security Council emphasized the importance of cooperation in repressing piracy through routine patrols to deter the crime, as well as collaborative action—after the pirates are caught—to bring them to justice. In the past, coordination on disposition and logistics issues associated with detainees unfolded haphazardly, but that could change with the resolution from the Security Council that strengthens multilateral expectations. Disposition and logistics assistance includes provision of medical care to those injured, conducting investigation of the incident, providing a venue for detention and prosecution of suspects, and arranging lodging and repatriation of crew members who invariably hail from disparate regions.

The Security Council resolution also solved one of the most vexing issues associated with piracy—that of Somali pirates capitalizing on the lack of government control over territorial waters by grabbing ships and hostages in international waters and then fleeing inside territorial boundaries to evade capture. Now, warships have a mechanism under the auspices of the Security Council to cooperate with the Transitional Federal Government of Somalia and conduct "hot pursuit" of pirates that seek sanctuary and refuge in Somalia's territorial sea. The resolution is a starting point for deterring piracy by increasing the risk associated with the crime. Once a vessel is seized, invariably it is taken to anchorage near the shore to await payment of ransom by the shipping company that owns the vessel. Under the Security Council resolution, pirates can no longer be certain that a rescue attempt will not be made during this time. Indeed, in the case of the *Golden Nori*, a Panamanian-flagged chemical tanker seized in 2007, the vessel was taken into Somalia's territorial waters. But British and U.S warships prevented the pirates from re-supplying the vessel, helping to force a peaceful resolution six weeks later.

Recent collaboration to develop international laws suppressing maritime piracy has exceeded the most optimistic predictions of even a few years ago, laying the groundwork for new authorities and partnerships. Collaboration is particularly vital because most of the ocean's surface is not under national jurisdiction, and no single nation has the naval capability to patrol effectively the enormous area impacted by piracy. Although the UN and the IMO have taken steps to broaden international legal authority available to suppress maritime piracy, much more can be done. The fight against piracy should be recalibrated to become even more effective. The next step requires a smarter approach to counter-piracy operations, logistics, and the legal endgame by developing agreements among the major shipping nations and regional states to enable real-time coordination for dealing with detainees, sorting out where they will be temporarily detained and the venue for prosecution.

The International Community Must Work with Africans to Combat Piracy

Michael L. Baker

Michael L. Baker was a 2009–2010 international affairs fellow at the Council on Foreign Relations, a Washington, DC, think tank, where he studied African political and maritime security issues. He also has served as a US Navy foreign area officer, focusing on West African engagements.

For nearly two years, international navies have policed the waters off Somalia to try to stamp out piracy. More than thirty vessels are deployed across the Indian Ocean and the Gulf of Aden under a wide range of banners, including NATO [North Atlantic Treaty Organization], U.S., European Union, and Chinese. Yet despite the size and sophistication of these international task forces, Somali pirates continue to expand operations.

According to the International Maritime Bureau, in the first half of 2010, Somali pirates have attacked ninety-one ships and taken control of twenty, and are getting closer to India's coastline. So while the number of attacks appear to be lower than last year (217 attacks and 47 successful hijackings for the whole of 2009), Somali piracy continues to represent a substantial threat to commercial shipping. The international community needs a new, more strategic approach to countering piracy based on building partnerships and trust with Africans both at sea and onshore.

The Somali Problem

Many commentators have noted that piracy is part of a greater problem—namely, the lack of a Somali state—and can only be

Michael L. Baker, "Building African Partnerships to Defeat Piracy," CFR.org, June 2010. Copyright © 2010 by Council on Foreign Relations. All rights reserved. Reproduced by permission.

solved by improving both governance and living conditions for Somalia's public. To achieve that the international community needs credible partners within Somalia. Yet the United States is reluctant to work with many Somali groups and has focused its efforts on bolstering Somalia's Transitional Federal Government (TFG). This endeavor has borne little fruit to date and is not likely to be useful when it comes to countering piracy, since the TFG has virtually no ability to change conditions in the northern autonomous region of Puntland.

Some Somalis in Puntland still stand to gain from the trickle-down effects of pirate wealth. It is also not unusual to hear Somalis talk about the negative effects of illegal foreign fishing or the dumping of waste off their coastline, causing them to view pirates as a champion of sorts. So long as these attitudes persist among average Somalis, it will be extremely difficult to stop piracy.

If the international community is going to be successful in its fight against piracy, it will therefore have to change the opinion of Somalis in Puntland by taking measures to build trust with the public and incorporate them as viable stakeholders in maritime governance and security to counter illegal fishing, dumping, and piracy.

The situation calls for a long-term, multifaceted approach at sea and onshore that establishes trust, protects and builds markets, and enforces laws (both national and international).

It is also not unusual to hear Somalis talk about the negative effects of illegal foreign fishing or the dumping of waste off their coastline, causing them to view pirates as a champion of sorts.

The African Union and several of its member states have publicly spurned piracy and have signed a code of conduct to repress piracy, commonly referred to as the "Djibouti Code of Conduct". But only Kenya and the Seychelles have taken any

notable action—by agreeing to receive and try captured pirates—and Africans are conspicuously absent from the joint
patrols. Meanwhile, behind closed doors, some African bu-
reaucrats and leaders decry piracy as an outside problem
plaguing the rest of the world but not Africa. They claim that
the international community expects Africa to solve piracy
while those same actors turn a blind eye toward illegal fishing
and dumping.

Global actors should respond to such sentiment by expanding their activities in areas where Africans have high interests and work on long-term approaches to improve African
participation in the maritime domain writ large. They should
use a robust partnership with Africans at sea to improve partnerships ashore and get at the core problem of the failed Somali state. And they should ensure that their African counter-
parts understand the real impact that piracy has on African
citizens.

Piracy's Impact on Africa

For starters, Africans who believe that piracy is primarily a
problem for Westerners are misguided. The costs of piracy are
passed on to consumers as shipping companies recoup the
majority of their losses through their protection and indemnity clauses, and insurance companies recoup their losses
through increased rates and policies. Recent reporting also in-
dicates that pirates are attacking ships carrying food items to
Somalia, causing shortages and increased prices for staple
items like rice and flour. World leaders should be sure that
their African interlocutors clearly grasp these realities.

The situation calls for a long-term, multifaceted approach
at sea and onshore that establishes trust, protects and builds
markets, and enforces laws (both national and international).
The international task forces in the Gulf of Aden and the Indian Ocean can play a strategic role in each of those three areas to change conditions on the ground in Somalia, but they

have to change the nature of their partnerships and expand their mandates. Fortunately, there are good examples in West and South Africa.

In March 2009, in the inaugural Southern Africa Joint Patrols, Kenya, Mozambique, South Africa, and Tanzania conducted combined patrols in the Indian Ocean on board the *Sarah Baartman*, a South African environmental protection ship. During the one-month operation, the team inspected forty-one vessels, levying ten fines and arresting six ships for violations of national maritime laws. The highlight of the operation was the seizure of one vessel in Tanzanian waters with over 300 tons of illegal tuna on board.

In June 2008, the United States Africa Command and Cape Verde's government initiated the African Maritime Law Enforcement Partnership (AMLEP). This operation puts African maritime boarding teams and police on board U.S. Coast Guard or U.S. Navy vessels to enforce African maritime law, AMLEP offers an operational platform for small African maritime forces, enabling them to extend their reach throughout their territorial seas and Exclusive Economic Zones. To date, AMLEP operations have focused on combating illegal fishing and countering illegal trafficking in West Africa. The last two operations resulted in five seizures of vessels illegally fishing in Sierra Leone's waters. Operations like the Southern Africa Joint Patrols—so far a one-time action—and AMLEP build trust through combining maritime law enforcement personnel from different countries on one vessel and operating at sea for extended periods of time. By conducting routine inspections of commercial and private ships, they achieve three distinct but interrelated goals: 1) build or enhance the capacity of African maritime law enforcement or security forces; 2) enforce regulations that support free and fair maritime markets; 3) seek and address the full range of maritime crime (drug-trafficking, smuggling, illegal fishing, illegal migration, and piracy).

A More Strategic Approach

The various task forces in the Gulf of Aden and Indian Ocean should put African seamen and boarding teams on their vessels to build partnerships, trust, and African capacity; and they should address the full range of illegal maritime activity in those waters.

Naval partnerships with African states would play an important role in reviving and improving the Somali fishing industry, a vital source of jobs and wealth.

Rather than simply reacting to Somali piracy, states should work to address the problems of governance both at sea and ashore through partnerships with Africans. The various naval task forces should put African seamen and boarding teams on their vessels to build partnerships, trust, and African capacity; and they should address the full range of illegal maritime activity in those waters. Existing models in South and West Africa prove that it is not difficult to take these steps. Such actions will deflate Somali claims that foreign powers only care about their own shipping interests while tacitly condoning the theft of Somali fish. Simultaneously, this approach will build African capacity to conduct similar missions in the future.

Furthermore, naval partnerships with African states would play an important role in reviving and improving the Somali fishing industry, a vital source of jobs and wealth. Such an approach would provide the international community an important strategic message that could eventually open doors with new partners ashore capable of returning law and order to Somalia as a whole and more likely to end Somali piracy in the long run.

Counterterrorism Measures Must Be Applied to Piracy

James Jay Carafano and Jon Rodeback

James Jay Carafano is director of the Douglas and Sarah Allison Center for Foreign Policy Studies at the Heritage Foundation, a conservative Washington, DC, think tank. Jon Rodeback is research editor at the Heritage Foundation.

Piracy is a growing threat to global commerce and is becoming a U.S. security issue, especially with the pirates' growing ties to international terrorism. Not only have ransom payments to pirates funded expanding piracy off the coasts of Somalia and driven up the costs of maritime commerce, but they may be supporting terrorist activities in the region and elsewhere as well.

At the very least, piracy is helping to perpetuate the lawlessness in Somalia. In February 2011, piracy took a deadly turn when Somalia pirates hijacked a yacht off Somalia and then killed the four people onboard—all of them Americans. Anti-piracy efforts to date have achieved some success, particularly in the Strait of Malacca, but they have failed to halt the spread of piracy in the Gulf of Aden and the Indian Ocean.

The U.S., in cooperation with other seagoing nations—an anti-piracy "coalition of the willing"—needs to move beyond defensive measures and start taking the fight to the pirates, attacking every aspect of the pirate networks. The U.S. and other countries should use every means at their disposal to deny the pirates any safe haven—geographical, financial, or legal—and bring them to justice wherever it is most convenient.

James Jay Carafano and Jon Rodeback, "Taking the Fight to the Pirates: Applying Counterterrorist Methods to the Threat of Piracy," *Heritage Foundation Backgrounder*, no. 2524, March 4, 2011. Copyright © 2011 by The Heritage Foundation. All rights reserved. Reproduced by permission.

Ties to Terrorism

In addition to aiding in lawlessness and other enterprises, it is thought that pirates are also supporting extremist organizations operating in northern and western Africa.

Al-Qaeda [terrorist network] leaders and publications clearly state that al-Qaeda seeks to [according to National Defense University researcher Andre Le Sage,] "oppose peace-keeping efforts in Muslim countries, notably Somalia and Sudan," and harm the global economy by disrupting oil production. Furthermore, [according to Le Sage,] "Somalia has long been a rear base for the East Africa al Qaeda (EAAQ) cell" that conducted the successful 1998 attacks on U.S. embassies. Rather than basing "its primary leaders or principal training camps" in Africa, al-Qaeda has established ties with local Islamist groups. Hizbul Islamia, a splinter group from Somali terrorist group Al-Itihad al-Islamia (AIAI), is "seeking to establish an Islamist state in Somalia," [continues Le Sage,] Harakat al-Shabab, another AIAI splinter, has been working with EAAQ to establish an Islamic state in the Horn of Africa.

The U.S., in cooperation with other seagoing nations . . . needs to move beyond defensive measures and start taking the fight to the pirates.

At first glance, the terrorist and pirate activities may seem unrelated, but terrorist organizations benefit from pirates in many ways. Al-Shabab benefits from the goods and weapons that pirates smuggle into various Somali ports. Somalia is also a port of entry into Africa for foreign fighters and a transit point for terrorists traveling to other countries, including those responsible for the March 2009 bombing in Yemen.

In turn, Islamist groups permit pirates to operate in Islamist-controlled areas. Pirates use the proceeds from hijacking and pilfering ships to pay suppliers. Potential terrorists and criminals use pirates not only as a means of transportation, but also as a source of financing and materials (e.g., weapons, drugs, and other materials in hijacked ships) that terrorists find useful.

Some experts have argued that these illegal organizations can operate in such proximity without cooperating to a significant degree and developing strong ties. In contrast, Admiral Mark Fox, Commander of U.S. Naval Forces Central Command, has observed:

> Al-Shabab is responsible for a lot of training activity and camps and that sort of thing in Somalia. . . . The pirates use these things. There cannot be a segregation between terrorist activity, in my mind, and counter piracy. We can't be passive and hopeful it doesn't happen.

Pirate Tactics

Somali pirates often go to sea in a "mother ship," which is usually a fishing vessel captured in a previous pirate attack. The mother ship enables the pirates to stay at sea longer and operate further away from Somalia than if they just used their skiffs. Earlier in this decade, they often used skiffs to launch attacks from land. The pirates also use the mother ship to scout for targets of opportunity.

Once a passing cargo ship has been spotted, the mother ship deploys two to four smaller high-speed vessels (skiffs), which flank the target and approach at high speed. To slow or stop the ship, pirates use various means of intimidation, including firing automatic weapons and rocket-propelled grenades. Once the target has slowed, a team of seven to 10 pirates boards the ship using ladders and grappling hooks and takes the ship and its crew hostage. The team of pirates is usually armed, and the small number of crewmen required to operate modern merchant ships (usually no more than a dozen) makes hijacking a ship relatively easy.

Once hijacked, larger cargo ships and their crews are often sailed to a pirate port in Somalia to await negotiation and payment of their ransom. Pirates also maintain networks of depots along coasts, where they can sell captured goods, re-arm, and resupply their ships. The network of depots also affords them the opportunity to communicate with spies in the region to obtain information about ships that may be passing through the area.

Profits from hijacked cargo are disbursed to the pirate suppliers, organizers, and investors who support the pirates during their time at sea. The illegal income may also benefit their clan members, including family and friends. The profits from piracy support the local economy, filtering through the community as pirates resupply and upgrade their vessels and weapons and as those in the network spend their wages.

Current Counterpiracy Efforts

Modern efforts to suppress piracy have met with mixed success. Piracy in the Strait of Malacca has declined significantly, but the Somali pirates have expanded their operations.

The Strait of Malacca. In 2004, there were 38 recorded pirate attacks in the Strait of Malacca, but only two incidents were reported in 2008 and another two in 2009. This is an example of successful regional cooperation and public-private cooperation under the Regional Cooperation Agreement on Combating Piracy and Armed Robbery Against Ships in Asia. Sixteen nations participate in that regional operation.

Gulf of Aden and the Western Indian Ocean. Piracy off Somalia has proven more difficult to address because the failed state of Somalia provides the perfect base from which to mount pirate activities. Local law enforcement is either non-existent or powerless against the Somali pirates, and international law largely protects the pirates from outside interference while on land. Compared with pirates in the Strait of

Malacca, the Somali pirates also have much more room to operate, from the Suez Canal to the west coast of India.

There are currently three major multinational anti-piracy missions near the Horn of Africa. Since November 2008, the European Union's [EU] Operation Atalanta has protected World Food Program vessels delivering food to Somalia and other ships in the region. NATO [North Atlantic Treaty Organization]'s Operation Ocean Shield has deployed warships in the region with a mandate to protect shipping until the end of 2012. Finally, Combined Task Force 151, a multinational task force established in January 2009, patrols the Gulf of Aden and the east coast of Somalia.

Even the U.N. [United Nations] Security Council has acknowledged the threat of Somali piracy and has repeatedly extended authorization for U.N. member states and regional organizations to take "all necessary means to repress acts of piracy and armed robbery at sea" in Somali territorial waters. This authorization for other states to violate the territorial waters of another state marks an unusual step and is *de facto* recognition that Somalia has no functioning government to control its territory.

The Legal Environment

Under customary international law, countries have long exercised universal jurisdiction over acts of piracy on the high seas: [As noted British jurist William Blackstone put it,] "As therefore [a pirate] has renounced all the benefits of society and government, and has reduced himself afresh to the savage state of nature, by declaring war against all mankind, all mankind must declare war against him." Essentially, any country can legally act against pirates outside national territorial waters, regardless of the pirate's "nationality" and the nationality of the vessel attacked by pirates. The U.S. Constitution specifically authorizes Congress to "define and punish piracies and felonies committed on the high seas, and offenses against the law of nations." In fact, piracy was a major impetus for the development of international law, the body of rules and customs that guide relations between countries.

The 1982 U.N. Convention on the Law of the Sea (UNCLOS) generally codified this understanding of universal jurisdiction and even expanded the definition of piracy, but in some ways it has complicated enforcement. [As law expert Eugene Kontorovich notes,] "In the classic law of nations, pirates were simultaneously criminals and military enemies." At sea, a pirate could be attacked and killed but was also subject to capture and trial by law, unlike a prisoner of war. Yet commonly accepted interpretations of UNCLOS and Article 3 of the Geneva Conventions have turned this historical practice on its head, providing [according to Kontorovich,] "pirates today [with] the protections of criminal defendants, as well as some of those of enemy prisoners, without the disabilities of either."

This has complicated the legal environment to the point that many foreign navies are reluctant to take pirates prisoner, much less prosecute them. In the first six months of 2010, EU and NATO naval forces captured and then released an estimated 700 pirates. More recently, Denmark released six pirates, who were captured attacking the container ship *Elly Maersk*, because [as stated by Danish reporter Bent Mikkelsen,] "there was not enough evidence for a conviction in a Danish court." This legal vacuum, in part, explains why Russia set 10 pirates adrift in the Indian Ocean on the flimsy excuse that it lacked [according to the BBC report,] "sufficient legal grounds to detain them." The freed pirates are presumed to have died at sea.

An Offensive Strategy Is Needed

A defensive strategy of trying to protect every ship that passes through high-risk zones, particularly in the Gulf of Aden and the western Indian Ocean, will almost certainly fail because there are too many vulnerable ships, too few law enforcement and military assets to protect them, and too many pirates. Furthermore, modern pirates, especially those based in Somalia, have demonstrated an impressive ability to adapt to and exploit the changing security environment.

Exploiting the Pirates' Vulnerabilities. To end the piracy threat off the Horn of Africa and in the western Indian Ocean, the U.S. and other countries should use their strengths to attack the Somali pirates at their weak points, including the pirates' profits, bases of operations, and manpower.

The U.S. and other countries should use their strengths to attack the Somali pirates at their weak points, including the pirates' profits, bases of operations, and manpower.

Money. The expansion of piracy is being driven by profit, whether that profit is sought for personal gain or for ideological reasons (e.g., financing terrorism). If piracy were not profitable at an acceptable level of risk to the pirates, there would be little or no piracy. Accordingly, the U.S. and other countries should strongly discourage the payment of ransoms and use all available tools of government to disrupt the pirates' financial transactions. Most of the ransom money that enters Somalia will eventually leave the country in some form to purchase goods unavailable in Somalia.

Consequently, the U.S. and other countries should try to make extracting ransoms, selling captured cargoes, and keeping the ransom money and proceeds of the sales increasingly difficult and expensive. If they succeed, the pirate enterprises will eventually respond to the changing economic incentives either by disbanding or by finding other more lucrative or less dangerous criminal activities.

Means. Piracy requires viable targets, pirate ships, and pirate ports. Pirates operate in the gaps in maritime enforcement, whether such enforcement is conducted by regular law enforcement or naval forces. By implementing basic, nonlethal defensive measures, the crew of a commercial ship can make its capture much more difficult. Even delaying capture dramatically increases the risk to the pirates by allowing naval forces to converge on pirates attacking the ship.

The mother ships that Somali pirates use are another potential weak point. Although a mother ship may initially appear to be an innocent commercial vessel, this facade will likely collapse under closer examination. A ship towing several skiffs or carrying the unique tools of piracy (e.g., weapons, grappling hooks, and hook ladders) is probably a pirate ship.

Somali pirates generally operate out of four Somali port towns: Caluula, Eyl, Hobyo, and Harardhere. These are geographical bottlenecks in pirate operations that anti-piracy forces can and should exploit.

Men. The nations of the world need to make piracy a riskier, more dangerous, and less profitable occupation. If potential recruits know that they run an increasingly high risk of never returning home, they will be less willing to join, and current pirates will be more inclined to retire while they are still alive and can enjoy their loot.

Selective targeting of pirate leaders, à la Predator attacks on terrorist leaders in Afghanistan and Pakistan, might also prove useful in persuading pirates to reconsider their career choices.

Knowing the Enemy. Much is already known about the pirate gangs operating out of Somalia. However, the U.S. and other countries need to expand both their situational awareness in the Indian Ocean and their understanding of how the pirates operate, especially as they react to new anti-piracy initiatives. Among other assets, unmanned aerial vehicles (UAVs), satellites, signals intelligence, human intelligence, and interrogations of captured pirates can help to fill in the knowledge and coverage gaps.

Additional Considerations

The problem of piracy offers no easy solutions. If it did, it would probably have ceased to be a problem given the assets that have already been deployed.

Hostages. The multinational forces should take reasonable precautions to avoid endangering the hundreds of hostages held by the Somali pirates. For example, direct attacks on pirate ports and depots along the coast are inadvisable because of the high probability of heavy casualties among hostages and civilians.

The long-term solution to Somali piracy is to establish effective governance of Somali territory and territorial waters.

However, the U.S. and other countries should not allow the existence of hostages to dictate their responses to piracy. They should continue to look for opportunities to rescue hostages without killing hostages or civilians.

Captured Pirates. One of the most difficult challenges in combating piracy is dealing with captured pirates. Russia's elegantly simple solution of setting them adrift at sea is not a viable option for the U.S. or EU countries. Until recently, Kenya had signed agreements with the United Kingdom and the U.S. to accept custody and try pirates. However, in 2010, Kenya stopped accepting custody of pirates.

Preferably, pirates would be tried in nearby countries or on board ships. Until Somalia has a viable government, most pirates should be prosecuted and imprisoned by other countries in the region. Judicious use of international aid to support these countries would be a good investment that would strengthen law and order in the region while dramatically reducing enforcement costs.

A Long-Term Solution. While the U.S. and its allies can make a pirate's life more difficult and shorter, the long-term solution to Somali piracy is to establish effective governance of Somali territory and territorial waters. Without safe havens from which to operate, most piracy would probably disappear.

> [We should go after pirates], their supply lines, and their financial transactions with "the same intensity [the coalition members] use when targeting terrorists."

In Somalia, efforts to build a functioning central government from the top down have failed by all accounts. Instead, efforts to bring order to Somalia should start small and work up. Building government up from the grassroots in Somalia offers some hope, but it will be long-term project. However, the disruption of piracy will severely disrupt the remains of the Somali economy, particularly since piracy has been one of the few growth industries in Somalia in recent years. When piracy collapses, it will affect many Somalis who are not directly involved in piracy and complicate matters for any nascent Somali government. Rebuilding the Somali economy will take time.

Targeting Pirates as Terrorists

Piracy has become a serious threat to international commerce, and the Somali pirates have been developing ties with Islamist terrorists in the region. Admiral Fox has the right idea in treating the pirates as terrorists and going after them, their supply lines, and their financial transactions with "the same intensity [the coalition members] use when targeting terrorists."

Military Action and Foreign Aid Must Be Used to Eliminate Pirate Sanctuaries

Bernd Debusmann

Bernd Debusmann is a columnist for Reuters, an international news agency.

In 2005, the average ransom paid for the release of a ship hijacked by Somali pirates was around $150,000. By the end of last year [2010], it stood at $5.4 million. That means revenues for the business of piracy more than doubled every year. The 2005 to 2010 percentage increase is a staggering 3,600 percent.

Catch and Release

The ransom numbers come from the One Earth Foundation, a U.S. think tank, and help explain why the business of piracy, probably the world's most profitable, has been expanding—despite an increased international naval presence in the waters hounded by Somali pirates, despite a string of plans to protect shipping, and despite increasingly exasperated statements from politicians and ship owners.

Talking about pirates off Somalia, who killed four Americans on February 22, [2011] U.S. Secretary of State Hillary Clinton said this week [mid-March 2011] that "I'm fed up with it." Piracy is moving up Washington's list of priorities, according to her. A few weeks earlier, Ban Ki-Moon, the United Nations Secretary General, noted that "piracy seems to be outpacing the efforts of the international community to stem it."

Ship owners agree. Early in March [2011], five of the world's largest maritime organizations, complaining that

Bernd Debusmann, "Why High-Seas Piracy Is Here to Stay," Reuters, March 4, 2011. www.blogs.reuters.com. Copyright © 2011 by Thomson Reuters. All rights reserved. Reproduced by permission.

"2,000 Somali pirates are hijacking the world's economy", launched an advertising campaign and a website (www.Save OurSeafarers.com) demanding tougher action. The group includes the International Chamber of Shipping, which represents about 80 percent of the world's merchant ships, and INTERTANKO, whose members operate most of the world's tankers.

In half page advertisements in leading newspapers, including the *Wall Street Journal*, the group noted that "even when caught red-handed, 80 percent of pirates are released to attack again."

The practice, known as "catch and release", figures in the risk-reward calculations of the piracy business, whose leaders are aware of the thicket of laws, regulations and jurisdictional ambiguities which has made arrest and prosecution of pirates difficult. There are no uniform rules of engagement for the warships on counter-piracy missions in the Gulf of Aden and the Indian ocean. By some definitions, an act of piracy does not begin until grappling hooks are thrown over the sides and the pirates start clambering up.

While the number of navy vessels on counter-piracy patrols has increased (there are about 30 warships on patrol now) so has the area threatened by pirates, who launch speedboats from mother ships up to a thousand miles from the Somali coast. So, the warships are looking for needles in a haystack.

The key to solving the problem is on land—the fact that Somalia, a failed state, is a sanctuary for pirates. No country is prepared to take action against that sanctuary.

An Enterprise Doomed to Failure

Which is why trying to end piracy purely with sea-borne operations looks like an enterprise doomed to failure. The key to solving the problem is on land—the fact that Somalia, a failed state, is a sanctuary for pirates. No country is prepared to take action against that sanctuary, where more than 800 seafarers are currently held hostage.

"The problem is being addressed right now only from the sea," Nikolas Gvosdev, a professor at the U.S. Naval War College, said in a recent radio discussion on piracy. "We are trying to deter attacks. We are trying to protect ships. But the problem lies on land. It lies in villages and port cities, in ungoverned spaces where . . . this is a profitable business. It is essentially the main driver for revenue in Somalia."

Donna Hopkins, the U.S. government's coordinator of Counter Piracy and Maritime Security, has described piracy as "deeply ingrained in the Somali economic and social structure" and said the problem would continue as long as there is no effective government to control territorial waters and the Somali coastline.

When might that happen? Don't hold your breath. Somalia has had no effective government since 1991 when the Communist dictatorship of Mohamed Siad Barre was toppled. In the two decades since then, the country has been torn by fighting between rival warlords and militias, an Ethiopian invasion to oust Islamists, and battles between militants linked to al Qaeda [terrorist network] and what passes for a government.

Pirates can be chased on the ocean, but piracy can only be eradicated on land.

In the process, Somalia earned the dubious distinction of being ranked the world's most corrupt country. It came dead last on the 2010 corruption perception index of 178 countries compiled by Transparency International, a watchdog group based in Berlin.

The longer the problem festers, the more difficult it is to resolve. "As pirates become richer, they become harder to dislodge," says Roger Middleton, the author of a report on piracy by Chatham House, a British think tank. "Pirates can be chased on the ocean, but piracy can only be eradicated on land."

So what to do? One way would be stepped up military action on land, following the example of a daring helicopter-born French commando raid in 2008 to capture pirates who had held 30 hostages from a French yacht. Another way would be to redouble international efforts to finally help Somalia establish an effective government to tackle the linked problems of piracy, poverty, hunger and war.

Both options require what the ship owners backing the Save Our Seafarers campaign say governments around the world lack—political will.

A Long-Term Piracy Solution Requires Addressing Somalia's Poverty and Politics

Rubrick Biegon

Rubrick Biegon is a policy consultant and journalist who is a frequent contributor to Foreign Policy in Focus, a project of the Institute for Policy Studies, a Washington, DC, think tank.

The recent spike in pirate attacks off the coast of Somalia has generated a great deal of international media attention, including news reports sprinkled with ubiquitous references to Long John Silver [a character in Robert Louis Stevenson's book *Treasure Island*], Jack Sparrow [a character in the *Pirates of the Caribbean* movies], and Captain Hook [a character in the story "Peter Pan"].

Commentators are quick to point out that, unlike these legendary fictional raiders, Somalia's modern pirates represent not only a very real menace to maritime security, but also a growing threat to international commerce. And yet, for all their swashbuckling swagger, we know little about the pirates themselves. The sensational nature of their crimes, while drawing the ire of the international community, has also ensured that the Somali pirates remain shrouded in mystery.

Increasing Numbers

On January 16, [2009,] the London-based International Maritime Bureau (IMB) released a report detailing the upsurge in piracy in 2008. Worldwide, the number of pirate attacks increased by 11%, an "unprecedented rise in maritime hijackings" the IMB attributed almost exclusively to an explosion of

Rubrick Biegon, "Somali Piracy and the International Response," Foreign Policy in Focus, January 29, 2009. www.fpif.org. Copyright © 2009 by Foreign Policy in Focus Global Affairs Commentary. All rights reserved. Reproduced by permission.

attacks in the Gulf of Aden, the stretch of the Arab Sea separating war-torn Somalia from Yemen. Of the 293 piratical incidents the IMB recorded for the year, 111 attacks occurred on the high seas surrounding Somalia's territorial waters. This represents a staggering annual increase of nearly 200% in the critical trade corridor linking the Suez Canal and the Indian Ocean.

As the hijackings have increased in number they have also become more sophisticated, enabling the pirates to seize larger targets. On September 25 [2008], Somali pirates captured the *MV Faina*, a Ukrainian ship transporting Soviet-era weaponry to Kenya. This was followed one month later by the hijacking of the *MV Sirius Star*, the largest ship ever captured by pirates. A Saudi-owned supertanker carrying approximately 2 billion barrels (about $100 million worth) of crude oil, the *MV Sirius Star* was finally released on January 9 for a $3 million ransom. However, the pirates continue to hold the *Faina* and its crew near the small port city of Eyl, located in Somalia's semi-autonomous Puntland region. All told, the Puntland-based pirates are believed to be holding at least a dozen seized vessels. Over 300 merchant mariners are being held hostage—though, it should be noted, their treatment has been less-than-barbaric by most accounts.

The increased threat of maritime piracy has heightened the shipping industry's financial concerns in the context of the global economic recession. Over 6.8 billion tons of goods are moved by sea annually in a global trade cycle worth $7.4 trillion, with up to 90% of international trade traveling by ship at some point. The wave of pirate attacks off the eastern coast of Africa has already had a major impact on global shipping patterns. Following the hijacking of the *Sirius Star*, for example, AP Moller-Maersk, Europe's largest shipping company, diverted its fleet of 50 oil tankers away from the Suez Canal towards the longer and more expensive route around the Cape of Good Hope. In addition to the massive ransoms that the shipping companies pay for the release of their vessels, the financial burdens associated with maritime piracy include, among other things, excess fuel costs, increased payroll costs, and higher insurance premiums.

Furthermore, due to the inherent volatility of commodity prices, particularly oil, high-profile incidents of maritime piracy can have economic impacts far beyond their immediate target. This phenomenon has been on display in Nigeria, for instance, where seaborne attacks by the Movement for the Emancipation of the Niger Delta (MEND) against international oil companies led to periodic spikes in the global price of crude. Given the fact that over 10% of the world's petroleum deliveries are trafficked through the Gulf of Aden, there's little doubt that the region's highly strategic location is a prime factor driving the international community's rapidly deepening response to the "scourge" of Somali-based piracy.

International Response

The Gulf of Aden is currently being patrolled by one of the largest anti-piracy flotillas in modern history. Organized as the Combined Maritime Forces, the United States-led coalition features warships from at least 20 different navies. Due to differing rules of engagement and the various legal complexities related to capturing, holding, and prosecuting pirates, the multilateral contingent has attempted to combat pirate attacks mainly through the sheer strength of its presence in the area. As one would expect, pirates tend to shy away from commercial vessels backed by a military escort, preferring instead to go after unprotected and thus more vulnerable targets.

Despite the robust size of the international community's anti-piracy fleet, however, the Somali pirates have grown increasingly brazen in recent months. On December 16 [2008], the same day the UN Security Council passed a resolution authorizing air and land strikes against pirates during "hot pursuit," Somali raiders attacked four more vessels in the Gulf of

Aden. To date, the bandits have remained relatively undeterred by the immense firepower that has been assembled to thwart their piratical efforts. Even China's unprecedented decision to send two destroyers to the region (the country's first far-flung naval deployment since the creation of the People's Republic in 1949) has failed to fully quell the attacks.

On January 8 [2009], the U.S. Navy announced the reorganization of the multilateral forces patrolling the Gulf of Aden. Through the establishment of Combined Task Force 151 (CTF-151), the United States and its partners have sought to strengthen the force's ability to deter and disrupt the pirates by freeing-up a section of the coalition forces to focus exclusively on pirate groups (leaving Combined Task Force 150 to focus on other destabilizing activities, such as drug smuggling and weapons trafficking). Tellingly, U.S. Vice Admiral Bill Gortney, the coalition's commander, cautioned that even the best efforts of the international navies involved in the task force will be insufficient in solving the problem of piracy in the Horn of Africa. Ultimately, if there is a solution to be found, it rests onshore, in the devastated Somali communities that have given rise to the pirates, and to which they return.

The Gulf of Aden is currently being patrolled by one of the largest anti-piracy flotillas in modern history.

Robbers or Robin Hoods?

In many ways, the Somali pirates exemplify what the British historian Eric Hobsbawm referred to as "social bandits," outlaws who, drawing on community support, use criminal methods to challenge prevailing hierarchies of power and wealth. One doesn't have to romanticize the pirates to see that there is a quasi-political element to their actions. As stated by the BBC [British Broadcasting Corporation], not only is piracy "socially acceptable" in Somalia, it's even become "fashionable . . . in a country where almost half the population needs food aid after

17 years of non-stop conflict." Even [Britain-based international newspaper] the *Economist* has likened the pirates to Robin Hoods—albeit somewhat dismissively.

In a country that ranks near the very bottom in virtually all socio-economic indicators, maritime piracy is far and away Somalia's most lucrative business.

Piracy in Somalia began because traditional coastal fishing became difficult after foreign fishing trawlers depleted local fish stocks. Desperate fishermen started attacking trawlers until the trawler crews fought back with heavy weapons, leading the local fishermen to turn to other types of commercial vessels. The pirates prefer to call themselves the Somali "coast guard," noting that, prior to the recent spate of hijackings, they organized themselves to defend their communities from overfishing and, according to several accounts, to protect Somalia's coastline from toxic dumping by foreign vessels.

In a country that ranks near the very bottom in virtually all socio-economic indicators, maritime piracy is far and away Somalia's most lucrative business. Ship owners are willing to pay millions for the release of their hijacked vessels. By most estimates, the pirates have taken in around $30 million in the past year, though the actual figure may be many times this amount. Kenya's foreign minister, for example, maintains that the pirates collected over $150 million in ransoms in 2008 alone, a sum that greatly exceeds the budgets of the country's balkanized regional governments.

At the local level, Somalis have championed the banditry by tolerating the pirates, providing them safe havens on shore. According to an article in *The Spectator* by Aidan Hartley, in Puntland, "the modern world's first genuine pirate state," the gangs of bandits are made up of "ordinary youths" who are more than willing to pay local merchants inflated prices for consumer goods. Well-organized and highly efficient, Somalia's pirates are opposed publicly only by the country's militant Islamic forces, including al-Shabaab, a terrorist organization with reported links to al-Qaeda [worldwide terrorist network]. A pirate leader known as Boyah has boasted that the raiders can't be stopped because, with officials so deeply involved in financing piracy, the government has no interest in cracking down on the bandits.

Looking Ahead

As Hartley says, "piracy is just one symptom of several ways— you can add gun-running and terrorism to the list—in which Somalia's crisis will lash out at the world in 2009." If the international community is to comprehensively address the crisis, its "first task is to understand the background."

Indeed, although an expanded and more aggressive naval presence in the Gulf of Aden may temporarily stem the tide of the growing pirate attacks, it hardly guarantees that, over the long-term, the chaos onshore will not again spill over into surrounding international waters. Besides being unsustainable from a logistical standpoint, the heightened military response, including the creation of Combined Task Force 151, will likely prove inadequate in addressing the root causes of the piracy itself. Both the U.S. Navy and the United Nations have acknowledged as much.

Clearly, the problem of Somali lawlessness at sea can't be addressed without attending to the ongoing crisis of Somali "statelessness" on land. Somalia's complex civil war dates to 1991 and, despite some positive steps in recent months, it's unlikely to be resolved in the immediate future. As U.S.-backed Ethiopian forces completed their withdrawal from Somalia on January 26, [2009,] ending a two-year occupation, their pullout was punctuated by several car bombs, including one in Mogadishu that killed 15 people.

As the violence continues to grab headlines, the international community would do well to remember that, while

Somalia's rampant sociopolitical instability provides its seafarers the opportunity to "flourish" as pirates, this instability is not the sole cause of the piracy boom. The characteristics of Somalia's "failed state" include dire economic conditions and crushing poverty, the harsh realities of life at the margins of the global economy. In the context of the chaotic political situation onshore, these conditions are as directly responsible for Somalia's pervasive piracy as the country's lack of an effective central government.

Supporting Somalia's Transitional Government Can Help Combat Piracy

Ken Menkhaus, John Prendergast, and Colin Thomas-Jensen

Ken Menkhaus is a professor of political science at Davidson College in North Carolina and a consultant for Enough, a project of the progressive group Center for American Progress that seeks to end genocide and other crimes against humanity. John Prendergast is a human rights activist, author, and the cofounder of the Enough Project. Colin Thomas-Jensen is an independent consultant who works on peace and security, conflict prevention, and human rights issues in sub-Saharan Africa.

For the first time in a long time, Americans are paying attention to what their government does in Somalia. Following last month's [April 2009's *Maersk Alabama*] hostage drama off the coast of Somalia, President Barack Obama is under increasing political pressure to address the threat of piracy in the Gulf of Aden. While short-term measures to curb pirate attacks are certainly necessary, the Obama administration must not allow the politics of the piracy problem to distract it from putting in place a long-term strategy to help Somalis forge a state that, with measured external support, can fight piracy, promote peace and reconciliation, and combat the threat of terrorism within its borders.

A Chance for Somalia

Historically, the international community's engagement with Somalia has more often made matters worse for both Somalis and external actors. Rather than invest in the time-consuming

Ken Menkhaus, John Prendergast, and Colin Thomas-Jensen, "Beyond Piracy: Next Steps to Stabilize Somalia," enoughproject.org, May 2009. Copyright © 2009 by Enough! A project to end genocide and crimes against humanity. All rights reserved. Reproduced by permission.

and undoubtedly frustrating process of helping Somalis forge consensus and build functioning state institutions, the United States, the United Nations [UN], and others have often backed governments based on narrow coalitions, or they have opted to partner with questionable nonstate actors in pursuit of near-term counterterrorism goals. This approach has frequently stoked further conflict and human rights abuses. Fourteen attempts in the past 19 years to reconstitute state authority in Somalia have failed, with ordinary Somalis bearing the brunt of these ill-advised, poorly executed, underresourced efforts. The latest effort—a five-year transition to democratic elections administered by a Transitional Federal Government, or TFG—nearly collapsed after two years of Ethiopian occupation and brutal counterinsurgency warfare. Ethiopia has now withdrawn, and a new, more broad-based TFG offers some hope, but the human rights crisis in Somalia remains acute and continues to deepen, the threat of Islamist extremism that the U.S.-backed incursion sought to neutralize persists, and piracy continues despite the deployment of a multinational armada.

Although the situation on the ground remains critical, we believe that the election of a new president, Sheikh Sharif Ahmed, and the establishment of a moderate Islamist government under his authority—"TFG version 2.0"—are potentially the best chance Somalia has had to pull itself out of nearly two decades of state collapse. For this effort to succeed, however, the Obama administration must resist calls for immediate, unilateral military action against terrorist and pirate targets on Somali soil and chart a new course in its approach to Somalia that privileges Somali-driven political processes, prioritizes inclusive governance, and respects Somali preferences. It not only needs to reshape U.S. policies toward Somalia, but must also press other external actors not to proceed with policies that are either flawed or intentionally destructive. . . .

Establishing Security

The immediate policy dilemma for international donors is one of sequencing: Must a security force first create conditions in which a civil government can survive and operate? Or must government authorities first establish a capacity to control security forces? Some may see a preference for checks and balances—and constraints on government security forces—as a normative agenda for human rights groups. But in Somalia it is also a cold realist calculation—abusive security forces will undermine, not protect, the TFG. And as in 2007 and 2008, such forces will strengthen public support for the shabaab and other opposition and extremist groups.

The election of a new president, Sheikh Sharif Ahmed, and the establishment of a moderate Islamist government . . . are potentially the best chance [for] Somalia.

The international community has already had one calamitous experience providing direct salary support to the TFG police in 2007 and 2008, when the government was under different leadership. The TFG police under then-President Abdullahi Yusuf committed grave human rights abuses against the Mogadishu population. The police commissioner during this period, Abdi Qeybdid, is still in place despite a track record of abusive behavior, lack of confidence among ordinary Somalis, and protests by human rights groups. Moreover, key branches of the transitional government—the judiciary, the interior ministry, and others—that are supposed to exercise oversight of police and other security forces are not yet functional. What the United Nations and some donors are proposing, then, is the strengthening of security forces in a context where the new government appears to lack the ability to hold them accountable. The U.N. secretary general's report is clear on this, identifying its strategic objective as [being] "to assist the TFG in creating security conditions in which the process of building the country's state institutions can take root."

The good news is that the TFG has made some progress on its own, and the international community may finally have a more credible partner than the previous TFG or its predecessors. A bank account has been established in [neighboring] Djibouti and an interdepartmental financial oversight body has been established to monitor the use of funds. Revenues from the port are reportedly now flowing to the central government, and although corruption has not been eliminated, it has been reduced. From these funds, the TFG announced this month [May 2009] that it had begun to pay salaries to its security forces. The key challenges for the United States and other external actors in the immediate term are to help to ensure that the TFG continues to pay its security forces, provides training and nonlethal equipment conditioned on their improved conduct, and establishes oversight mechanisms to ensure that funding does not support abusive forces or political score-settling.

Threats Facing the TFG

This daunting task is further complicated by the diversity of security threats facing the TFG, which include the following:

Insurgency by the shabaab and other radical groups.

The shabaab and other Islamic extremist movements in Somalia are an existential threat to the TFG and a major security concern for neighboring states and the West. As noted above, these extremist groups have lost much of their credibility in Somali circles now that Ethiopian occupying forces have withdrawn and the old TFG leadership has been replaced with new, moderate Islamist leaders. A portion of the shabaab— some argue most of the movement—are not ideologically committed hardliners, but rather tactical allies who could be negotiated with and brought into an expanding TFG power-sharing circle. If this group can be successfully weaned from the shabaab through negotiations, it would leave the recalcitrant hardliners exposed and weakened, and easier to defeat outright.

This is the two-pronged approach that President Sharif and his supporters are seeking to employ, and the TFG has reportedly already enjoyed some successes in pulling some armed groups away from the insurgency. The most important contribution the international community can make to this effort is to protect and expand political space for Sharif to negotiate;—even with individuals who might raise eyebrows in some corners. Ethiopia's security concerns are especially important to address in this regard. The United States and its allies must avoid the temptation to arbitrarily "redline" individuals and groups to whom Sharif will attempt to reach out. The acceptability of Somali armed opposition groups should be judged principally on their positions on a few core positions: Do they accept peaceful coexistence with their neighbors, especially Ethiopia? Do they reject affiliation and alliance with Al Qaeda? Do they renounce terrorist attacks and assassinations against domestic rivals and foreigners?

The shabaab and other Islamic extremist movements in Somalia are an existential threat to the [Somali government] and a major security concern for neighboring states and the West.

Even as it negotiates with part of the insurgency, the TFG will unavoidably have to fight to defeat the most hardline, foreign-backed wing of the shabaab. Direct external aid to TFG security forces is seen by many as unavoidable if the TFG is to defeat the hardliners and expand its authority in south and central Somalia, and the United Nations has asked donors to provide training, equipment, and stipends to the emerging TFG security forces. However, this places the United Nations and other external actors again in the position of a direct backer of one party in an ongoing civil war, a fact which contributes significantly to the targeting of international humanitarian aid workers by insurgents. External donors must be very clear about what they are doing if providing direct support to national security forces: They are choosing sides in a war.

Fragmentation of ad hoc militia.

The TFG has forged alliances and understandings with a range of local, mainly clan-based militias that have resisted the shabaab encroachment but that remain outside the TFG military. Bringing these groups into the formal TFG national security forces is a high priority, as they otherwise are vulnerable to defection to opposition groups and pose a potential armed obstacle to extension of TFG authority. To maintain these fragile alliances the TFG primarily needs cash to provide regular salaries. This should mainly be the responsibility of the TFG, not external donors. External donors should ensure that their funding does not provide salary support for clan paramilitaries, which are largely unaccountable.

Criminal violence and lack of public order.

Reducing criminality and establishing public order is a critical matter of legitimacy and credibility for the TFG in the eyes of the Somali public, and it is the principal yardstick that Somalis will use to assess the TFG's performance. A more effective police force is a necessary first step. The international community already has established police support, and is likely to provide stipends as well, but the burden rests with the TFG to ensure that the police are a source of order and not predation. Under the old TFG, the police were a menace to the public. Until Police Commissioner Abdi Qeybdid is removed from office, it is not clear that citizens of Mogadishu will have any confidence in the police force. International donors must press hard for accountability in the ranks of the Somali police as a precondition for aid.

The TFG is likely to relax rules on the operation of private security forces employed by businesses, which in the past have been important sources of security for neighborhoods adjacent to the business compounds. Additionally, the TFG may opt to encourage the re-establishment of nonradical, local Islamic courts, which were the foundation for the dramatic improvements in security under the Islamic Courts Union in 2006. Under the courts' brief rule, Somalis were willing to trade some of their personal freedoms for greater security. Donor states can play a constructive role by protecting political space for Sheikh Sharif and his government to pursue this option if they so choose, rather than reacting in alarm at the prospect of courts based on sharia [Muslim] law. At the same time, donors can support Somali-driven efforts to reduce the incompatibilities of sharia court proceedings and rulings with international judicial and human rights standards.

Piracy

The lowest order of threat to the TFG, the Somali people, the region, and the United States is actually the security item enjoying the greatest attention right now—piracy. Even so, the continued epidemic of piracy off the Somali coast is a problem and a test of the capacity of the TFG to extend its authority. Proposals to provide external assistance to the TFG for the establishment of a coast guard are premature, do not reflect the security priorities of the Somali people, and are unlikely to work. Indeed, training up coast guard officers could easily produce unintended consequences, as that new skill set will be more valuable in the piracy sector than in the public sector, producing defections from the coast guard. A more appropriate approach for the TFG will be to tackle piracy onshore. That will require time, funds, and extensive negotiations. External actors will have only limited roles to play in this internal Somali process.

Antipiracy measures would attract much greater support among Somalis if those efforts were accompanied by international action to end illegal fishing off Somalia's coast. Like the shabaab during the Ethiopian occupation, pirates have managed to cloak their criminal agenda beneath a veil of Somali nationalism. Although illegal fishing has undoubtedly decreased due to the effectiveness of Somali pirates, international commercial fishing boats have for years violated Somalia's territorial integrity and severely disrupted local Somali livelihoods.

The Obama administration should more deeply engage in Somalia's state reconstruction.

Upending the Status Quo

Given the significant national security interests that the United States has in Somalia with respect to counterterrorism, and the international political and commercial pressure generated due to piracy, the Obama administration should more deeply engage in Somalia's state reconstruction. The United States should appoint a senior diplomat along with a small diplomatic team to work with the U.N. mediation team. The American officials can provide focused, low-key support to this process of state reconstruction through the TFG. If this support is too visible or forceful, it will undermine President Sharif's efforts to reach out to disaffected clans and constituencies. In this space, the United States should work within the already established International Contact Group to maintain the focus on the transition and help ensure that President Sharif does not embark on a failed attempt at empire-building like so many before him.

The immediate priorities and recommendations for the United States should be the following:

1. Improve security: Support locally owned efforts to improve security and public order and reduce the threat posed by armed insurgents.

Somalia's most urgent need is unquestionably improved security. There are multiple security threats in Somalia, each of which requires a distinct response. Some security threats in the country are amenable to carefully calibrated external support—others are not. In all cases, local ownership of security policies is essential if those responses are to be sustainable, effective, and viewed in the eyes of local communities as legitimate. External aid is important, but it must not be allowed to overtake local responsibility to finance essential security operations. Moreover, direct support to the Transitional Security Forces must be conditioned on increasing inclusiveness of the TFG and effective steps to curb human rights abuses, including a commitment to investigate allegations of abuse and removal of officials implicated in serious abuses. The United States and other donors should establish oversight mechanisms under the auspices of the Joint Security Committee and AMISOM [African Union Mission in Somalia] and must be prepared to halt funding if, as was the case last year, TFG forces engage in widespread human rights violations and other forms of criminal behavior.

2. End impunity: Support Somali efforts to seek justice for war crimes and end a culture of impunity.

The Ethiopian intervention in late 2006 calcified a brutal insurgency that in turn provoked a heavy-handed and vicious counterinsurgency campaign. Without fear of punishment, all sides committed atrocities against civilians. Continued impunity is an affront to the victims and fuel for further conflict. A necessary first step is a credible investigation of crimes committed. As a permanent member of the U.N. Security Council, the United States should call for a U.N. Commission of Inquiry to investigate and document war crimes and crimes against humanity. Ultimately the question of how to hold perpetrators accountable must be answered by Somalis themselves, but a credible external investigation must occur to begin the process.

3. Focus on the transition and governance: Help President Sharif refocus on transitional tasks and improve governance in order to enlarge participation in the political process and defuse armed opposition as Somalia prepares for possible elections in 2011.

Under former President Abdullahi Yusuf, the TFG ignored the "T" (transition). Yusuf and his allies (including the Ethiopians) sought to destroy their enemies without building functioning Somali institutions or advancing key transitional tasks. The success of the transition now depends on whether President Sharif can establish credible, inclusive, and consultative national commissions to complete the transition.

As with transitional governments in other settings, the TFG will face complex problems related to constitutional choices on systems of representation, central and local government division of labor, checks and balances, and many other matters that will have a powerful impact on the question of "who rules" in Somalia in the future. It will also face daunting technical challenges with regard to other key transitional tasks, especially those related to the work of the electoral commission. Here the outside world has considerable experience and expertise that can be offered to Somali representatives. Again, donors must be careful not to erode Somali ownership of decision making on these matters by overloading the transitional process with outside consultants and preset templates that may not fit in a Somali political setting.

4. Manage external spoilers: Somalia is a theater for regional meddling and proxy conflict, and the United States must seek to end cross-border adventurism and neutralize sources of support for groups inside Somalia seeking to undermine the peace process.

Eritrea, Libya, Qatar, and Iran, among others, are actively supporting groups that oppose the TFG, and the Obama administration should construct a diplomatic strategy to erode that support. The Security Council has already authorized sanctions against individuals and groups that obstruct the peace process, and as an immediate first step the United States should work with other members of the Security Council to build consensus for sanctions against those individuals and groups identified by the U.N. group of experts to be implemented if they become spoilers to the peace process.

Ethiopia's cautious support for Sheikh Sharif is promising, but there will be great temptation for Ethiopia to intervene again if the shabaab and other extremist elements make further gains, or if the TFG's outreach to the opposition includes figures Ethiopia deems unacceptable. Renewed Ethiopian military activities in Somalia would undermine and likely collapse the TFG and fuel the insurgency. Simmering tensions between Ethiopia and Eritrea continue to destabilize the subregion and undermine Somalis' state-building efforts. The United States should resume serious efforts to fully implement the Ethiopia-Eritrea peace deal, demarcate the Ethiopia/Eritrea border, and normalize relations between the two countries. Without a resolution of the Ethiopian-Eritrean impasse, Somalia is likely to remain a site of ongoing proxy war between the two.

In fighting terrorism on land and piracy at sea, U.S. national security interests will be better secured if we aligned ourselves more with the interest of most Somalis in better security and effective governance.

Helping Somalia

Somalia has become the poster child for transnational threats emanating from Africa. By sea, pirates much more dangerous than their predecessors from centuries past prowl the Indian Ocean and Red Sea waterways and make tens of millions of dollars in ransom. By land, extremist militias connected to Al Qaeda units ensure that Somalia remains anarchic and the only country in the world without a functioning central government.

In fighting terrorism on land and piracy at sea, U.S. national security interests will be better secured if we aligned ourselves more with the interest of most Somalis in better security and effective governance. Helping to build the house and using the back door will be much more effective than barging into the front door of a house that has yet to be built.

Organizations to Contact

The editors have compiled the following list of organizations concerned with the issues debated in this book. The descriptions are derived from materials provided by the organizations. All have publications or information available for interested readers. The list was compiled on the date of publication of the present volume; the information provided here may change. Be aware that many organizations take several weeks or longer to respond to inquiries, so allow as much time as possible.

Cargo Security International (CSI)
Petrospot Ltd., Petrospot House, Somerville Court
Trinity Way, Adderbury, Oxfordshire   OX7 3SN
    United Kingdom
+44 1295 814455 • fax: +44 1295 814466
e-mail: info@cargosecurity.com
website: www.cargosecurityinternational.com

Cargo Security International is a website published by Petrospot Limited, a publishing, training, and events organization that provides information resources for the transportation, energy, and maritime industries. The CSI website provides information and intelligence on security-related commercial and governmental initiatives to transportation and security professionals, including updates on maritime piracy. A bimonthly magazine, *Cargo Security International*, is available on the site. There is also a section devoted to piracy, with numerous articles about the subject. Recent articles include: "Global Piracy Watch: New Anti-piracy Service Protects Vessels in Dangerous Waters" and "Global Piracy Watch: IMB Reports Almost 100% Increase in Piracy Attacks."

Contact Group on Piracy Off the Coast of Somalia (CGPCS)
Counter Piracy and Maritime Security
Bureau of Political-Military Affairs (PM/CPMS)
US Department of State, 2025 E St. NW, Suite NW8090

Washington, DC   20006
(202) 453-9309
e-mail: hopkinsdl@state.gov
website: www.state.gov/t/pm/ppa/piracy/contactgroup

The Contact Group on Piracy Off the Coast of Somalia is a voluntary, ad hoc international forum created on January 14, 2009, pursuant to United Nations Security Council Resolution 1851. CGPCS brings together countries, organizations, and industry groups to coordinate political, military, and other efforts to bring an end to piracy off the coast of Somalia and to ensure that pirates are prosecuted. Nearly sixty countries and several international organizations participate in the group, including the African Union, the Arab League, the European Union, the International Maritime Organization, the North Atlantic Treaty Organization, and various departments and agencies of the United Nations. The CGPCS website provides press releases on the group's activities and links to other organizations and entities involved in antipiracy work.

Federation of American Scientists
1725 DeSales St. NW, 6th Floor, Washington, DC   20036
(202) 546-3300 • fax: (202) 675-1010
e-mail: fas@fas.org
website: www.fas.org

The Federation of American Scientists is an independent, nonpartisan think tank and membership organization dedicated to providing rigorous, objective, evidence-based analysis and practical policy recommendations on national and international security issues connected to applied science and technology. The group's website provides relevant articles on piracy, including: "Piracy: A Legal Definition" and "Piracy Off the Horn of Africa."

The Heritage Foundation
214 Massachusetts Ave. NE, Washington, DC   20002-4999
(202) 546-4400
website: www.heritage.org

The Heritage Foundation is a research and educational institution that seeks to promote conservative public policies based on the principles of free enterprise, limited government, individual freedom, traditional American values, and a strong national defense. The group transmits its research and ideas primarily to members of Congress, key congressional staff members, policymakers in the executive branch, the nation's news media, and the academic and policy communities. Its website contains numerous publications on the topic of piracy. Examples include "Another Challenge for the Administration: Piracy in the Gulf of Aden," "Stopping Piracy Matters," and "Options for Combating Piracy in Somalia."

International Maritime Bureau (IMB)
ICC Commercial Crime Services, Cinnabar Wharf
26 Wapping High St., London   E1W 1NG
   United Kingdom
+44 (0)207 423 6960 • fax: +44 (0)207 423 6961
e-mail: imb@icc-ccs.org
website: www.icc-ccs.org

The International Maritime Bureau, a division of the International Chamber of Commerce (ICC), is a nonprofit organization founded to fight against all types of maritime crime. IMB's main goal is to protect the integrity of international trade. The IMB operates the Piracy Reporting Centre (PRC), which tracks actual and attempted pirate attacks worldwide and tries to raise awareness within the shipping industry of the areas and ports at high risk for attacks. The PRC works closely with various governments and law enforcement agencies and is involved in information sharing in an attempt to reduce and ultimately eradicate this piracy. The PRC section of the IMB website provides advice for shipowners, piracy news and data, and a weekly piracy report listing specific episodes of piracy.

International Maritime Organization (IMO)
4 Albert Embankment, London   SE1 7SR
   United Kingdom

+44 (0)207 735 7611 • fax: +44 (0)207 587 3210
e-mail: MaritimeKnowledgeCentre@imo.org
website: www.imo.org

The International Maritime Organization is the United Nations agency responsible for the safety and security of shipping and the prevention of marine pollution by ships. The IMO's Maritime Knowledge Centre maintains collections of publications on various topics, including maritime safety, as well as piracy laws, reports, and statistics.

Interpol
General Secretariat 200, quai Charles de Gaulle, Lyon   69006
    France
fax: +33 (0)4 72 44 71 63
website: www.interpol.com

Interpol is the world's largest international police organization, made up of nearly two hundred member countries. It seeks to facilitate international police cooperation in order to prevent or combat various types of international crime. Interpol's involvement in the fight against international terrorism includes maritime piracy. The Interpol website produces a list of publications related to this topic, including, "European Union Decision Endorses Central Role of Interpol Against Maritime Piracy Off Somalia" and "Interpol Maritime Piracy Working Group Aims to Enhance International Police Collaboration."

Overseas Security Advisory Council (OSAC)
Bureau of Diplomatic Security, US Department of State
Washington, DC   20522-2008
(571) 345-2223 • fax: (571) 345-2238
website: www.osac.gov

The Overseas Security Advisory Council, part of the US State Department, was established to promote cooperation between the State Department and private sector businesses on issues of security worldwide. Its creation was the result of the increase in terrorism over the last twenty-five years and the threat against US interests overseas. OSAC produces weekly and monthly reports on international maritime piracy, and its website provides links to organizations involved in maritime security. The website also contains news articles and other publications on piracy. Examples include "Spanish Court Sentences Somali Pirates to 439 Years" and "Somalia: Seafarers Threaten Boycott over Piracy."

US Institute of Peace
2301 Constitution Ave. NW, Washington, DC   20037
(202) 457-1700 • fax: (202) 429-6063
website: www.usip.org

The US Institute of Peace is an independent, nonpartisan, national institution established and funded by Congress. Its goals are to help prevent and resolve violent international conflicts; promote post-conflict stability and development; and increase conflict management capacity, tools, and intellectual capital worldwide. Its website contains various publications on the subject of piracy, including "Counting the Costs of Somali Piracy" and "Piracy and the Crisis in Somalia: Somali Perspectives."

Bibliography

Books

D.R. Burgess   *The World for Ransom: Piracy Is Terrorism, Terrorism Is Piracy.* Amherst, NY: Prometheus Books, 2010.

John S. Burnett   *Dangerous Waters: Modern Piracy and Terror on the High Seas.* New York: Dutton, 2002.

Nigel Cawthorne   *Pirates of the 21st Century: How Modern-Day Buccaneers Are Terrorising the World's Oceans.* London, United Kingdom: John Blake, 2011.

Peter Chalk   *The Maritime Dimension of International Security: Terrorism, Piracy, and Challenges for the United States.* Santa Monica, CA: RAND, 2008.

Peter H. Eichstaedt   *Pirate State: Inside Somalia's Terrorism at Sea.* Chicago, IL: Lawrence Hill Books, 2010.

Colin Freeman   *Kidnapped: Life as a Hostage on Somalia's Pirate Coast.* London, United Kingdom: Monday Books, 2011.

Robin Geiss and
Anna Petrig

*Piracy and Armed Robbery at Sea:
The Legal Framework for
Counter-Piracy Operations in Somalia
and the Gulf of Aden.* New York:
Oxford University Press, 2011.

Daniel
Heller-Roazen

*The Enemy of All: Piracy and the Law
of Nations.* New Castle, PA: Zone,
2009.

Angus Konstam

Piracy: The Complete History. New
York: Osprey, 2008.

James Kraska

*Contemporary Maritime Piracy:
International Law, Strategy, and
Diplomacy at Sea.* Santa Barbara, CA:
Praeger, 2011.

Gabriel Kuhn

*Life Under the Jolly Roger: Reflections
on Golden Age Piracy.* Oakland, CA:
PM Press, 2010.

Martin N.
Murphy

*Piracy, Terrorism and Irregular
Warfare at Sea: Navies Confront the
21st Century.* New York: Routledge,
2011.

Martin N.
Murphy

*Somalia, the New Barbary? Piracy and
Islam in the Horn of Africa.* New
York: Columbia University Press,
2011.

Martin N.
Murphy

*Small Boats, Weak States, Dirty
Money: Piracy and Maritime
Terrorism in the Modern World.* New
York: Columbia University Press,
2010.

John C. Payne — *Piracy Today: Fighting Villainy on the High Seas.* Dobbs Ferry, NY: Sheridan House, 2010.

Michael R. Pierce — *Piracy Survival Guide: A Cruisers Guide to Dealing with Piracy.* Millington, TN: Celeste, 2011.

Brooks Tenney — *The Incense Coast: Piracy Around the Horn of Africa.* Mustang, OK: Trafford, 2010.

Periodicals and Internet Sources

Stephen Askins — "Piracy—US Presidential Order on Payment of Ransoms and Recent Developments," *Somali Pirates*, March 12, 2011. www.somalipirates.org.

Baird Maritime — "Piracy: Record Hostage-Taking in 2010, Says IMB," January 19, 2011. www.bairdmaritime.com.

Michael L. Baker — "Smarter Measures in Fight Against Piracy," Council on Foreign Relations, December 10, 2010. www.cfr.org.

BBC — "Piracy 'Cannot Be Solved at Sea,'" June 23, 2009.

Max Boot — "Fight Off, Don't Pay Off, Pirates," *Commentary*, January 24, 2011. www.commentarymagazine.com.

Douglas R. Burgess Jr.
"Piracy Is Terrorism," *New York Times*, December 5, 2008. www.nytimes.com.

Jia Cheng
"Anti-piracy Training Helping Ship Crews Thwart Attacks," *Global Times*, November 23, 2010. http://military .globaltimes.cn.

CNN
"Despite U.S. Policy, Nothing Stops Ransom Payment, Expert Says," April 8, 2009. http://articles.cnn.com.

Economist
"Somali Piracy: At Sea: Piracy Off the Coast of Somalia Is Getting Worse. Time to Act," February 3, 2011. www.economist.com.

Duncan Gardham
"Government 'Complacent' Over Pirates Link to Terrorists," *Daily Telegraph* (London, United Kingdom), July 21, 2009. www.telegraph.co.uk.

Jeffrey Gettleman
"Suddenly, a Rise in Piracy's Price," *New York Times*, February 26, 2011. www.nytimes.com.

Jon Henley
"All at Sea," *Guardian* (Manchester, United Kingdom), November 19, 2008. www.guardian.co.uk.

Pauline Jelinek
"Admiral: U.S. Should Pursue Pirate Ransoms," *Navy Times*, April 16, 2010. www.navytimes.com.

Mary Kimani   "Stopping High-Seas Piracy: More
                     Regional Cooperation Needed for
                     Peace and Security," United Nations
                     Africa Renewal, 2009. www.un.org.

MSNBC   "Pirate Attacks Hit an All-Time High
                     Worldwide: 'Dramatic Increase in the
                     Violence and Techniques' Seen from
                     Somali Pirates," April 14, 2011.
                     www.msnbc.msn.com.

Bambang Hartadi   "Extending Cooperation to Combat
Nugroho   Sea Piracy," *Jakarta Post* (Indonesia),
                     April 25, 2011.
                     www.thejakartapost.com.

Mallory Simon   "Report: 2010 Was Worst Year Yet for
                     Piracy on High Seas," CNN *This Just
                     In* (blog), January 19, 2011.
                     http://news.blogs.cnn.com.

Terra Daily   "Technology to Combat Piracy in the
                     High Seas," December 2, 2009.
                     www.terradaily.com.

Vivienne Walt   "Why the Somali Pirates Keep
                     Getting Their Ransoms," *Time*, April
                     20, 2009. www.time.com.

Lesley Anne   "Pieces of Eight: An Appraisal of U.S.
Warner   Counterpiracy Options in the Horn
                     of Africa," *Naval War College Review*,
                     Spring 2010. www.usnwc.edu.

Sharon   "Intrigue, Brinksmanship Woven into
Weinberger   Hidden World of Pirate Ransoms,"
                     AOL News, March 27, 2011.
                     www.aolnews.com.

Index

A

Abdikarim, Mahad Omar, 87

Adam, Jean and Scott, 92

Adams, John, 18, 119

Africa
    Cape of Good Hope, 30, 56, 151, 179
    East Africa, 39, 54, 152, 156, 165
    North Africa, 21, 120, 134
    piracy in, 29, 155, 161–163
    South Africa, 131, 162
    West Africa, 38, 162–163
    See also Horn of Africa region; Somalia

African Maritime Law Enforcement Partnership (AMLEP), 162

African Union, 25, 65, 160

African Union Mission in Somalia (AMISOM), 141, 193

Ahmed, Abdullahi, 96

Ahmed, Mohamed, 69–71

AK-47 automatic rifles, 28, 34, 44, 92, 129, 155

Al-Itihad al-Islamia (AIAI), 165

al-Mujahideen terrorists, 67

al-Qaeda terrorists
    goals of, 165
    ideological motivations of, 95
    link to al-Shabaab terrorists, 69, 80, 84, 183, 189
    piracy links to, 90, 176
    purchasing pirate captives, 105
    in Somalia, 63, 195

al-Shabaab terrorists
    benefits to, 165

financing tactics of, 87–89
    insurgency by, 188–189
    as jihadists, 66–70
    link to al-Qaeda terrorists, 69, 80, 84, 183, 189
    pirate attacks by, 89–90
    purchasing pirate captives, 105
    Somali pirates and, 65–70, 85–90, 145

Al Shebah terrorist group, 113

Alakrana (fishing boat), 123

Algerian pirates, 17–18, 152

Ali, Mohamud Salad, 92

Ali, Sugule, 100–101

Ali Osman Atto militia, 89

Allianz Group, 54–55

Allied Provider (Operation), 22

American Revolution, 17

Anti-piracy efforts
    against Haradheere pirates, 171
    against hostage taking, 172
    by NATO, 39, 150, 168
    by Obama, Barack (administration), 95–96
    by TFG, 41
    training for, 103
    by United Nations, 21, 61, 134, 157, 168, 180–181
    by United States (U.S.), 22–23, 115–117, 139–140
    See also Counter-piracy measures

Aon Risk Services, 55

AP Moller-Maersk (shipping company), 179

Arab League, 25

207